FROM MASCULINE TO FEMININE AND ALL POINTS IN BETWEEN

A Practical Guide for Transvestites, Cross-Dressers,
Transgenderists, Transsexuals, or Those Who Choose to
Develop a More Feminine Image . . . and for All Others
Who Are Interested, Concerned, or Curious

Copyright 1990 by
Different Path Press
Box 251
Harvard Square
Cambridge, MA 02238

Library of Congress Catalog Card Number: 90-081153
ISBN 0-9626262-0-1

ACKNOWLEDGMENTS

The list of people who have been helpful in the formation of the ideas contained in this book . . . and helpful to me along the way in my search for self, is so long that this space doesn't allow inclusion of all.

But I would feel remiss in not mentioning some special friends who have made this book, and all it encompasses, possible.

The late Christine Jorgensen allowed us all to realize that we really could take control of our lives; Dr. Virginia Prince, "mother" of the transvestism movement and another person whose courage in facing the cold realities of life to-be-lived-as-one-chooses opened up the closet for literally hundreds of thousands of those who followed her; Ari Kane, whose creation of the Outreach Institute and its famous Fantasia Fair made personal experiences for me, my "coming out" so much easier; Dr. Harry Benjamin, whose early work on the subject of transvestism and transsexualism gave medical credence to the subject as well as personal advice to me which eventually had a great effect on my future "T" activities; Merissa Sherrill Lynn, Organizer of The International Foundation for Gender Education, and editor of Tapestry, certainly the premiere organization and the leading magazine in the field; Niela Miller, therapist, whose advice and patience have been so meaningful in the creation of my feminine persona and in the development of this book and many of its concepts; Leslie McGrath, humanitarian, whose love of the world and all peoples in it continues to influence many, many lives each day; The Reverend Kim K. Crawford Harvie, Universalist Unitarian Minister, whose love of humankind and encouragement for self-expression have opened the eyes of tolerance for so many; and to special friends who have helped all along the way, including Dr. Jayne Thomas, Dr. Nancy Ledins, Dr. Dave Smith, Margie Erhart, Kay Baker, Eleanor Cohen, Anne Wolfe, and Eva Wolf.

TABLE OF CONTENTS

Understanding Yourself

One of the first discoveries that any person involved in and around the cross dressing/transvestite - transsexual world will make is that titles are confusing.

Yet everyone who deals with this culture seems to wish to have some sort of common terminology so that others will be able to focus on similar problems—and opportunities— with a shared frame of reference.

Some feel that the term "transvestite" is dated...that the term "cross-dresser" is more appropriate.

The word "transsexual" is also confusing. Just how far along the road must a person be to be "officially" designated a transsexual?

Is a transsexual one who considers herself pre-operative...is she to be called a true transsexual? Or must the operation actually be completed before a person is labeled a transsexual?

And who does the labeling? Does a transsexual label herself a transsexual? Or is that name given only by the medical community?

Is the label "transsexual" wishful thinking on the part of someone who is "only" a cross-dresser?

The more that is written on this subject, the more confusing it gets.

In an attempt to clarify terms, Merissa Sherrill Lynn, chairperson of the International Foundation for Gender Education, has compiled a "Definition of Terms Commonly Used in the Transvestite/Transsexual Community." In her words:

This is not a directory of universally accepted definitions for terms. I have years of input and evaluation and re-evaluation and compromise before we can produce such a directory. Instead, treat this directory as 'food for thought', a tool to help you understand how the terms are most commonly used, how they interface, and to develop your own 'meaning' for them.

We have divided the terms into two catagories, 'Influential Terms' and 'Primary Terms'. The primary terms are the traditional ones ('transvestite', 'transsexual', etc.). The influential terms are terms that are commonly used in the TV/TS Community, and affect our understanding of the primary terms.

Terms mean different things to different people. I can give you solid authoritative definitions (personal opinions), to help you understand what you mean when you use a term, and to be able to comunicate that meaning to others. It is also to help you understand others. In short, this directory is more about communications than definitions.

Influential Terms

TERM/CATEGORY:

Even though 'term' and 'category' mean pretty much the same thing, I'm making a distinction because 'term' implies an idea or an expression, and tends to be more flexible, while 'category' implies a classification, and tends to be less flexible, and a little more dangerous to the person being categorized. People within the TV/TS Community are vulnerable to being categorized. Terms are used to describe phenomena, and categories are used to pigeon-hole them.

BIOLOGY/PSYCHOLOGY/ SOCIOLOGY/LANGUAGE:

When it comes to understanding the nature of the transvestite-transsexual phenomena, not knowing what terms and categories belong to which science creates the most problems. Biology is a life science. 'Sex', 'male', 'female', and 'man'

or 'woman' as modes of being are not biological terms. (See below.)

Psychology is a science of the mind. What do we think and feel? Why do we act the way that we do? How do we perceive ourselves as human beings? How do we deal with unwanted feelings such as guilt, lack of self-respect, anger, etc.? Most of the categories (especially those ending with -ism) used by the TV/TS Community were coined by psychologists.

Sociology is the science of human beings living together. How do we want to be perceived in public? How do we want to be treated? How do we treat others? What are our responsibilities to our community, and what are our community's responsibilities to us? How do we act in public?

Language is a collection of words created out of the imagination of man to describe his environment and to communicate. It is very important to understand the difference between words as labels describing qualities of Nature, and words as concepts and value judgments created out of the imagination of man. 'Female' is a label describing a biological fact, while 'feminine' is a value assigned to a quality such as 'gentle' or 'pink'.

To put it in terms relevant to this directory, Biology is concerned with our biological make-up, what our body is and how it works. It is concerned with physical fact. Psychology and sociology are more concerned with what we think, what we say, how we feel, how we act, how we dress, how we inter-act with others, and why. They are not concerned with physical fact. Language is concerned with the meaning of words, which as I've already stated, is vulnerable to subjective interpretation. Some words just identify physical facts, some are value judgments, and some are concepts. It is important to know which is which.

We have an opinion. (We warned you.) Biological fact is natural fact, and no amount of chemicals, or a good surgeon's knife is going to change that fact. As far as biology is concerned, a human being is little more than a biological specimen, and not a "person". Virtually everything that makes a human being a "person" is based in psychology and sociology. Psychology and sociology are artificial sciences, influenced perhaps, but not based on biological fact. They are actually more influenced by philosophy and language than by biology. 'Language' is an artificial creation, a collection of words created by the imagination of man to describe his environment and to communicate. 'Language' is not a natural fact. Morality and ethics are artificial creations, not natural facts. Thinking is artificial, acting is artificial, being a person is artificial. In short, biological fact is real, but when it comes to people being people, not very relevant. Psychology and sociology are artificial, but when it comes to people being people, completely relevant.

HELPING PROFESSIONAL:

Most people think of 'helping professionals' as therapists, doctors, social workers, educators, consultants, etc. who are researchers, or have members of the TV/TS Community or their 'significant others' as clients.

I have a problem with that definition. What is 'therapy'? What does a consultant consult about? Can someone providing a support service such as a beautician, or cosmetologist, or electrologist, or a member of the world's oldest profession be called a helping professional? Can anyone who offers professional services to the TV/TS Community in any way be called a 'helping professional'? My feeling is, "Yes they can!" It is then up to us to categorize.

SEX/GENDER:

One of the greatest sources of confusion is not understanding the difference between 'sex' and 'gender'.

'Sex' is a biological term dividing a species into either male or female, usually based on sex chromosomes (XX = female, XY = male, XXY = whatever). 'Sexual gratification' is also a biological term. Sex is sex; a biological fact, or a physical act. 'Sex' says nothing about the person other than describing a person's chromosomes and biological function (gestation, lactation, menstruation, impregnation, XX vs XY, whether we stand or sit when we poo, etc). "Sexual gratification' says nothing about how one achieves sexual gratification, and God knows, there are a lot of ways to achieve it.

'Gender' is much more complicated. Originally 'gender' was a grammatical tool, a classification by which to give the proper inflection to words (masculine, feminine, neuter). 'Gender' has now taken on a much broader meaning. It has been taken out of the grammatical context, and applied to life itself. Now 'gender' is to 'masculine' and 'feminine' what 'sex' is to 'male' and 'female'. 'Gender' is a bundle of value judgments (this is masculine—that is feminine).

SEXUAL FUNCTION/GENDER ROLE:

Another problem area is confusing one's sex with one's role in life. 'Sex' is a matter of biological fact. A person is born male or female. 'Role' is, as the dictionary puts it, the character an actor plays in a performance. In life you are the actor, and the character you play in society is your role'. That 'character' you play may be, and frequently is, severely limiting, or fundamentally incompatible with your identity as a person. If so, you have a problem, but it is a gender problem, not a sex problem.

Sexual function is all those biological things that go along with being male or female, and is never a 'role'. On the other hand, gender role is a mode of being, a way to be, how we express ourselves as people, how we act, how we dress, how we feel, how we think. Unfortunately, we tend to assign gender roles according to sex (who gets the blue blanket, who gets the pink, act like a man; like a woman), and we all know that those assigned roles are not necessarily compatible with our preferred roles.

SEXUAL IDENTITY/ GENDER IDENTITY/ GENDER EXPRESSION

Sexual identity is whether or not a person perceives him/herself to be male or female (see 'male' and 'female'). The problem arises when a male perceives himself to be female, and vice versa. What sex are we? You are and always will be the sex with which you were born. Can we change our sex? No! The best you can hope for is through chemistry and surgery you can function as the opposite sex, and for legal and practical purposes, that's good enough. (see 'sexual dysphoria').

Gender identity is whether or not a person perceives him/herself to be a man or woman (see 'man' and 'woman'). The problem arises when a male perceives

himself to be a woman, and vice versa. Notice we said man or woman, and not male or female. The difference is important. Male and female are biological terms, while man and woman as they are used here are modes of being, ways to be, which are based on psychology and sociology rather than biology. (see 'gender dysphoria')

Sexual identity is a 'transsexual' issue and may involve sexual re-assignment surgery, but may not involve cross-dressing. Gender identity is a 'transgender' issue and does not involve surgery, but almost always involves cross-dressing.

Gender expression is the term nearest and dearest to the hearts of most cross-dressers. In the TV/TS Community gender expression is males expressing their femininity and females expressing their masculinity using cross-dressing as a tool. Gender expression transcends the TV/TS Community, but that's another issue.

GENDER EUPHORIA/DYSPHORIA/ SEXUAL EUPHORIA/DYSPHORIA:

Each year these fancy terms seem to grow in popularity, especially among the helping professionals, and people who like big words. Granted 'dysphoria' is more impressive than the word 'unhappy' or 'uncomfortable', but they basically mean the same thing. (Euphoria means 'happy', or sense of well being).

Gender dysphoria/euphoria = Unhappy/happy with one's socially and culturally assigned gender role.

Sexual dysphoria/ euphoria = Unhappy/ happy with one's biological make-up or sex.

An understanding of these terms is especially important when it comes to deciding whether or not someone is a proper candidate for sexual reassignment (some people prefer 'corrective') surgery. Being unhappy with one's gender role is one thing. Being unhappy with one's sex is something completely different, and usually decides a person's identity, whether or not a person is just going to be a recreational cross-dresser, live as a transgenderist, or change sex.

MALE/FEMALE:

'Male' and 'female' are biological terms, identified by various biological criteria such as sexual function, XX or XY chromosomes, etc. (See 'Sex')

Notice we said 'male' and 'female' are defined by biological criteria, and not by any psychological or sociological criteria. Any discussion on how a male or a female is supposed to feel, or act, or dress, is simply inappropriate. (Chromosomes don't feel, act, or dress up.)

MASCULINE/FEMININE:

"Masculine' and 'feminine' are gender terms. In Nature there is no such thing as masculinity and femininity. 'Masculinity' and 'femininity' are value judgments, words used to identify and qualify qualities of Nature. In other words, what is masculine or feminine is strictly a matter of prevailing opinion, subject to change, and not a matter of biological fact.

Those qualities of Nature that we label masculine or feminine are inherent in all things, including both males and females. The tragedy is that many people cannot accept that it is natural for males to have feminine qualities, and females to have masculine qualities. It would be unnatural if males or females didn't have these qualities, or worse, denied it.

MAN/WOMAN:

'Man' and 'woman' are defined both in biological and psycho-sociological terms.

The biological definitions are simple: 'Man' = adult male, and 'woman' = adult female. The biological definitions of 'man' or 'woman' are sexual definitions. As we mentioned earlier, these definitions may be perfectly correct, but not very relevant. They say nothing about a person's identity, how he/she feels, or his/her lifestyle.

Psycho/sociological definitions for 'man' and 'woman' are not so simple. These definitions determine a person's identity—whether or not they perceive themselves to be a man or a woman. They also define the criterion for what constitutes a man or a woman, the dress code, the gender role, the code of conduct, what a man or woman is supposed to think, and how they are supposed to feel. The problem is, nobody can agree on the definitions. 'Society' says one thing, yet each individual who makes up that society says another. Every place that a person would look to find a role model says something different—the movies, the family, religion, the community, the media, teen idols.

In short, if a person is looking for an acceptable psycho/sociological definition of what a 'man' or 'woman' is, the answer is frighteningly simple—there isn't any.

Sexual definitions of what constitute a 'man' or a 'woman' are irrelevant. The only relevant definitions for 'man' and 'woman' are psycho/sociological—yet there aren't any, none that are generally accepted, anyway. The answer to this dilemma is, it is the responsibility of each individual to decide for himself what constitutes a 'man' or a 'woman'.

Whether or not a person considers him or herself to be a 'man' or a 'woman' is a matter of personal identity, a matter of personal gender (not sexual) identity. The only valid judge as to whether or not an individual considers him or herself to be a 'man' or a 'woman' is that individual, and the only relevant basis upon which to make that judgment is gender, and not sex.

SEXUAL PREFERENCE:

Sexual preference is being mentioned in this article because of the prevailing public opinion that people who cross-dress are 'gay', and the big ado made by cross-dressers who insist they aren't. Neither is the case, and the resulting problems such as fear, guilt, and rejection are pointless, counterproductive, and dangerous. People have enough problems trying to cope with gender expression and identity without being handicapped by being identified with sexual categories. However, it is important to understand how sex relates to the cross-dressing/transsexual phenomenon.

It is incorrect to think of people as just plain 'sexual'. Animals are capable of a sexual response. Human beings are animals. Being human, people are capable of abstracting or embroidering what triggers that sexual response. Human beings are capable of being sexually 'turned on' by virtually anyone, anything, anywhere, and any time. People are multi-sexual. It is not unnatural for a male human being to be sexually 'turned on' by seeing, touching, or wearing 'feminine' clothing, or seeing himself wearing that clothing. All it is, is one more variation of the natural human sexual condition.

We separate just plain 'sexual' from the other 'sexuals' (heterosexual, homosexual, bisexual) because 'sexual' is a description of the human condition, while the other sexuals define what constitutes a sex object, fantasies, the sex act itself, or a lifestyle. With the exception of 'sexual', the sexual categories define phenomena, not people.

There is no need in this article to define 'heterosexual', 'homosexual', or 'bisexual'. Ambisexual means bisexual, and trisexual means 'will try anything sexual'. The most practical of these terms is 'trisexual', for that only describes someone who likes engaging in sex. Sex is sex, and a person who likes sex is sexual, and all other categories are irrelevant.

Sex plays a prominent (and in some cases a dominant) role in the cross-dressing experience. The role sex plays in the cross-dressing experience is not important. What is important is someone having a prejudice against a particular sexual category, labeling a person according to that sexual category, then inflicting their personal prejudice upon that person. Cross-dressers have a terrible tendency to do this to themselves (resulting in guilt and self-hatred), to other cross-dressers (resulting in the rejection of others, the isolation from others, and the fear and hatred of others), and make themselves vulnerable to the prejudices of others (resulting in the fear of social reprisal, and withdrawal). All anyone needs to do is understand the nature of sex, and respect other people's preferences, and these pointless never-ending tragedies would come to a halt.

TURN-ON:

A turn-on is anything that excites, or creates a state of euphoria, or ecstasy. Most people associate 'turn-on' with sex, but it can also be sensual or emotional.

We all know that for most people cross-dressing is a turn-on. But what many people fail to acknowledge is that cross-dressing is not necessarily a 'sexual' turn-on.

FETISHISM:

Basically speaking, a fetish is an object or part of the body that, although not sexual itself, elicits an erotic response. Fetishism is the condition in which erotic feelings are exited by a non-sexual object. The cross-dressing world has a plethora of fetish items, and plenty of fetishists to enjoy them. (E.g., lingerie, high-heeled shoes, corsets, maids' outfits, virtually anything and everything).

Most people who cross-dress started because it was a sexual turn-on. (Most people also deny it.) The largest group of people within the TV-TS Community are fetishists. It has been implied by some that the mainstream cross-dresser is non-sexual. That's not true. The mainstream cross-dresser is sexual. The sexual motivation is like being in the first grade. That's where you start. Eventually you graduate to other rewards such as feeling happy, feeling pretty, narcissism, a sense of harmony, peace of mind, identity, escapism, the freedom to give and receive affection and love without sexual overtones, etc. The list is endless. However, the primary reward for the mainstream cross-dresser is sex. What does that say? It says most cross-dressers are still in the first grade.

The mainstream cross-dresser is usually very closeted, and keeps the adult bookstores and mail-order houses very happy. (The manager of Boston's Lane Bryant store told me they estimated that 30% of their business was by men for

men.) Most TV/TS organizations are non-sexual. Their members are usually people who have graduated from the first grade. Since the 'movers and shakers' of the TV/TS Community are usually members of an organization, it can be said that the mainstream mover and shaker is non-sexual . . . but not completely.

Why is cross-dressing such a sexual turn-on? If you find out, let me know.

FANTASIST:

'Fantasist' is a term growing in popularity, especially among helping professionals. The term solves the age-old problem of what to call a transvestite who doesn't cross-dress. Since 'transvestite' means 'cross-dress', and cross-dressing describes the activity and not the desire or compulsion, you can't very well call them transvestites. (However, if transvestism describes the desire and not the activity, then you can call them transvestites, but may not want to.) Then you have those who enjoy the fantasy of cross-dressing or role reversal, but don't necessarily enjoy or have the desire to actually cross-dress. There are those who fantasize about transsexualism, but aren't transsexuals. In addition, there are those who can't separate fact from fantasy.

'Fantasist' is a catch-all term, like 'cross-dresser'.

A cross-dresser is someone who cross-dresses for whatever reason. A fantasist is someone who 'fantasizes' about whatever, but doesn't 'do' whatever.

SIGNIFICANT OTHER (SO):

'Significant other,' or 'SO', is a term growing in popularity. It identifies a person who is not a member of the TV/TS Community, but is directly affected by one who is (e.g., a wife, fiancee, or close friend).

PASSING/BEING READ:

Passing' means being accepted by strangers as a member of the opposite sex.

'Being read' means not being accepted by strangers as a member of the opposite sex. (Beware of teen-age girls and 5-year-olds.)

NORMAL/DEVIANT:

'Normal' (norm) is a statistical term meaning 'average'. It is also a generally accepted standard or model. Cross-dressing is considered abnormal because it does not conform to that standard, but, that standard is constantly changing. Who knows, maybe some day cross-dressing will be considered 'normal'. (We hope not. Normal is boring. We like being different, and we like other people who are also different. We don't like people who think everybody should be normal. What we dislike even more are people who think normal is good and abnormal is bad. The norm is only an average, a standard,and no moral judgment is implied.)

'Deviant' is a statistical deviation from the norm. Again, no moral judgment is implied. Cross-dressing is deviant because it deviates from the norm, and we're deviant persons—and proud of it.

(As a footnote, when someone accuses Virginia Prince of being abnormal, she replies that she is statistically unusual, as were all great people in history, including Jesus Christ. Hurrah for Virginia!)

MENTAL ILLNESS:

Mental illness is being mentioned here because according to the third edition of the American Psychological Association's Diagnostic Statistical Manual (DSM-III) transvestism and transsexualism are still being carried as mental illnesses. The damage caused by that kind of stigma is staggering. The Gay Community was successful in having that stigma removed from homosexuality, and there is a movement afoot (albeit a small movement) to have it removed from transvestism and transsexualism.

PERSONA/ ANIMA/ ANIMUS:

In Jungian psychology, the theory is that the human psyche contains both masculine and feminine characteristics, and that the primordial drive of the psyche is towards wholeness. However, through the socialization process (role models, education, etc.) a person develops an identification with his or her sex,and represses those elements of the psyche which manifest the opposite sex. That identification with one's sex is called the 'persona'.

'Anima' is the suppressed or submerged feminine aspect of a man.

'Animus' is the suppressed or submerged masculine aspect of a woman.

We mention this because of the idea that all human beings, both male and female, have inherent masculine and feminine qualities, and that the natural tendency is towards wholeness. It is an idea that has been with us at least since the Vedas, which were written over 5,000 years ago, and is a fundamental element of Eastern philosophy (Yin and Yang, and all that), and is gaining popularity with Western philosophers and psychologists. Also, the idea that human beings have a natural tendency towards wholeness is very relevant to gender expression, for a male or female to express one's femininity or masculinity through cross-dressing. You will be hearing a lot more of 'persona', 'anima', and 'animus'.

II PRIMARY TERMS TRANSVESTITE/ TRANSSEXUAL (TV/TS) COMMUNITY:

We use 'TV/TS Community' to mean an identifiable group of people who cross-dress wholly or in part for what-ever reasons, and those persons for whom gender identity is an issue. It can also include anyone who wishes to identify with that Community. The act of 'cross-dressing' and 'gender identity' are the primary unifying factors, and services and affiliations are the secondary unifying factors. It does not exclude people on the basis of sex, sexual preference, personal identity, or extent of cross-dressing activity.

Let me stress that the above definition is my definition. There is an enormous amount of debate as to whether or not we should call it the 'TV/TS Community', and where we should draw the line as to who is a member and who is not. Here are a few of the arguments and counter-arguments:

1A) Change the name. the word 'transvestite' has negative and clinical connotations. The word 'cross-dressing' (CD) would be much better.

1B) Don't change the name. The word 'trans-vest' means cross-dress, and is more recognizable, so to change would unnecessarily muddy the waters.

2A) Change the name. Since the term 'androgyne' (AN) is more closely related to androgyny than cross-dressing, the Community should be called the 'CD/TS/AN Community'.

2B) Don't change the name. Androgynes use cross-dressing as a tool for achieving the 'harmonious whole', which makes them cross-dressers like everyone else. Again, why unnecessarily muddy the waters?

3A) The TV-TS Community must be exclusive. Since we are trying to take ourselves seriously, and are dealing with gender identity and expression and not sex, sexually oriented organizations and fetishists should not be included.

3B) The TV-TS Community must be inclusive. Cross-dressing is a continuous thread from fetishistic cross-dressing, to theatrical cross-dressing, to recreational cross-dressing, to transgenderism, to transsexualism. The organizations and services are so intertwined and the human overlap so great that you cannot possibly cut off one whole segment of that thread without damaging our ability to serve our community as a whole.

4A) Commercial and professional services should be included. Since we state in our constitutions that we cater to cross-dressers and transsexuals and those persons affected by and serving them, commercial and professional services and significant others should also be included.

4B) Commercial and professional services should be excluded. People who chose to identify with the TV/TS Community are members of that Community. Commercial and professional services and significant others do not generally identify with the Community. It is up to the individual as to whether or not they are members.

We have no 'accepted' definition for

'TV/TS Community'. We don't even have an accepted name. The term 'community' can be used to identify any special interest group (TS Community, SO Community, Watermelon-Seed-Spitting Community, you name it). We still have much work to do in defining ourselves, and our limits.

PARACULTURE:

The revolt against the word 'transvestite' has increased the popularity of the word 'paraculture'. 'Para-' means 'beside,' or 'along side of', implying that 'paraculture' is another culture, parallel to or alongside of culture—a culture within a culture.

Most people who use the word 'paraculture', use it to replace 'TV/TS Community'. Other people use it to describe not only the TV/TS Community, but the TV/TS Community as it spills out into society as a whole, engulfing helping professionals, commercial services, and persons directly affected by the Community.

We believe the word 'paraculture' creates more problems than it solves. Very few people know what the word is intended to mean, or how to use it. (Refer back to language and communications—know what the speaker means.) Most listeners will simply take the word out of context and make up their own definitions. The word is inevitably misunderstood or in need of additional explanation. Some people, myself included, find the word confusing and unnecessary. You may feel differently.

TRANSVESTITE (TV):

'Transvestite' (coined by Dr. Mangus Hirschfeld in 1910) is used to describe a person who wears clothing usually considered appropriate for the opposite sex. Unfortunately the word takes on a clinical guise, implying compulsive or sexual behavior, as though it were a disease or perversion. (It is neither a disease nor a perversion.) To make matters worse, most dictionaries still define transvestism as a manifestation of homosexuality. (That's wrong!!!! In fact the ratio of heterosexuality is higher among people who cross-dress than it is among the population in general.) 'Trans-vest' means nothing more than 'cross-dress'. It is in itself an innocent term, but it is very easy to understand why so many people who cross-dress (myself included) do not want to be identified with that word. The initials 'TV' for some reason do not carry the same negative connotations the word 'transvestite' does. Many people (myself included) who absolutely abhor the word 'transvestite', have no qualms whatever with being called a 'TV', or being identified with the 'TV/TS' Community. Also, the initials 'TV' are convenient to use, and readily identifiable.

EONISM:

Chevalier Charles D'Eon was a celebrated 18th century French transvestite. He was a spy for King Louis XV, and was hired as a 'lady in waiting' in the court of Czarina Elizabeth of Russia. He then served with distinction in the French army and was an accomplished swordsman. In 1762 he was sent on a spy mission to London where his penchant for women's clothing convinced people that he was in fact a woman. Only after his death in 1810 did they discover that he was really a man.

Until Dr. Hirschfeld coined the term 'transvestite', 'eonism' was used to describe men who wore women's clothing. It is still popular, and the Chevalier D'Eon still remains a remarkable historical character.

CROSS-DRESSER (CD):

'Cross-dresser' is used to describe a person who wears clothing usually considered appropriate for the opposite sex. The only difference between 'cross-dresser' and 'transvestite' is that 'transvestite' implies a psychological condition (compulsion), while 'cross-dresser' implies voluntary behavior. Most people who cross-dress (myself included) would rather be identified with the word 'cross-dresser' than 'transvestite'.

"Are you a transvestite?" "ABSOLUTELY NOT!!! I just enjoy cross-dressing."

Besides being an easy term with which to be identified, it also has the advantage of being vague. Since 'cross-dressing' is an activity, it includes everybody who cross-dresses for whatever reasons, and says nothing whatever about anybody. It's so vague and so meaningless it's perfectly useful. One can bandy the term about with absolute impunity, without hurting anyone's feelings or endangering anyone's identity.

It's a wonderful term—so non-controversial, and so safe! It's also a little boring, but what's a little boredom compared to safety?

DRAG/ DRAG QUEEN/STREET QUEEN/
SHE-MALE/SPIT DRAG/
FEMALE IMPERSONATOR-IMPRESSIONIST:

Rumor has it that the term 'drag' was coined by Shakespeare. In Shakespeare's day the female roles in a play were performed by men, and 'drag' was an acronym meaning Dressed As a Girl. The term was a theatrical term then, and is predominantly a theatrical term now, and implies a theatrical, showy, camp, exotic, or high glamour image.

Being 'in drag' is like being 'in costume'. It implies nothing about a person's sexual preference or inclination towards cross-dressing. (That is an important safety valve for those people who take their cross-dressing seriously, but don't want anyone to know they take their cross-dressing seriously.)

'Drag': Cross-dressing in glamourous, or campy, or exotic, or erotic attire ('high drag'), or conservatively ('low drag'). Usually drag is identified with 'high drag'.

'Drag queen': Usually a cross-dresser who prefers the drag image. Also, the term 'drag queen' is usually identified with the Gay Community.

'Street queen': Usually a drag queen who also hustles—a prostitute.

'She-male': Usually a gay male who lives full time as a woman; a gay transgenderist.

'Spit-drag': Usually cross-dressing as a joke, quite often a male In high drag sporting a moustache or beard.

'Female impersonator/impressionist': Usually a professional entertainer who performs 'in drag'. Impersonators are also associated with 'drag queen', so many entertainers prefer the term 'impressionist' in attempt to disassociate themselves from the 'drag queen' image, and to add some dignity to their profession.

There was a time when 'drag' and 'cross-dressing' meant virtually the same thing. However, since most cross-dressers do not consider themselves to be in costume, are not gay, and certainly not hookers.

TRANSGENDER (TG):

It used to be that a 'transgenderist' was a person who could express him or herself comfortably in both masculine and feminine terms. It was easier for a cross-dresser to identify with 'transgenderist' because the term did not carry the compulsive or sexual implications as did the term 'transvestite', and was far more specific than 'cross-dresser'.

Recently, however, the term 'transgenderist' has come more and more to mean a person of one sex living entirely in the gender role generally considered appropriate for the opposite sex (cross-living). Most people who consider themselves to be transgenderists do not want or need sexual reassignment surgery, and do not identify with 'transvestite'.

Most people who once identified with 'transgenderist', but do not cross-live, now opt for 'cross-dresser', 'femmiphile', or 'androgyne'.

FEMMIPHILE (FP):

'Femmiphile' was a term coined by Dr. Virginia Prince (founder of Chevalier Publications, and the Foundation for Personality Expression [FPE]—now the Society for the Second Self [Tri-Ess]). FPE was an organization for avowed 'heterosexual' males who enjoyed 'cross-dressing'. The intention was to provide a term that applies to this category. Fem-, meaning female or feminine, was combined with -phile, meaning lover. 'Femmiphile' consequently meant 'lover of the feminine'.

Unfortunately '-phile' is a suffix used mostly in professional circles, and carries psychotic overtones. For that reason most people shied away from identifying with the term. However, the term was created for the heterosexual cross-dresser, and because of the sexual or (even worse) with the 'homosexual' implications of 'transvestite', and the unacceptable simplicity of 'cross-dresser', and with the change in the meaning of 'transgender', and the confusion of 'androgyne', the word 'femmiphile' has made a comeback.

(Needless to say, though, the intellectual free spirits of the cross-dressing world are trying to come up with a better word.)

TRANSSEXUAL (TS)/ NEW MAN/NEW WOMAN:

The term 'transsexual' is sometimes used to describe a person in transition—working towards sexual reassignment surgery. (Rather than 'reassignment surgery' a growing number of people prefer the term 'corrective surgery'.) 'Transsexual' is sometimes used to describe a person who has completed her surgery (although many post-operative "T"s prefer 'new man' or 'new woman', or even 'man' or 'woman').

The most practical use of the term 'transsexual' is to describe someone whose 'gender' identity (their identity of themselves as a human being) is fundamentally and irrevocably incompatible with their 'sex', (biological make-up) regardless of whether or not they have taken any steps towards reassignment ('reconstructive') surgery.

The basic difference between a transvestite and a transsexual is that a TV is mostly interested in gender expression, and a TS is mostly interested in gender identity. For most TVs, the clothes themselves are very important. For most TSs, clothes are a way to reinforce their identity. That is a fundamental difference.

BI-GENDER TRANSSEXUAL:

'Bi-gender transsexual' is a term gaining popularity, especially in California. It is used to define those persons who see themselves as transsexually inclined, but still work as males, socialize as females (or vice versa), and do not plan to have sexual reassignment surgery.

The term 'bi-gender' was chosen because the individual's identity of him or herself as a person is stable (a man or a woman), but he or she lives in both gender roles. He or she also plans to continue doing so.

ANDROGYNE (AN):

'Androgyne' is the current 'in' word. 'Androgyne' was derived from andro-, meaning male, or man, and gyne-, meaning female, or woman. Philosophically, 'androgyne' found its roots in 'androgyny'. Modern androgyny is based on the ancient Far Eastern concept of the duality of the universe (Yin, Yang), with modern variations by psychologist C. G. Jung. Jung introduced the terms 'anima', which is the hidden feminine principle in men, and 'animus', which is the hidden masculine principle in women.

In the cross-dressing world 'androgyne' has come to mean using cross-dressing as a tool with which a man can express his femininity and a woman can express her masculinity. However, 'Androgyne' means a great deal more than using cross-dressing as a tool. It means harmony, rather, the sense of harmony, the harmonious balance between one's masculinity and femininity.

Yin and Yang (whose symbol is the well-known interlocking teardrops) is an ancient Chinese religious concept. 'Yin' is negative, dark, and feminine. 'Yang' is positive, bright, and masculine. (We think

that they had that backwards, but who am we to criticize ancient religions?) The Yin and Yang are inherent in, and influence the destinies of all things. The embodiment of the Yin and Yang was considered an ideal. With it went a sense of oneness, a sense of harmonious oneness with the universe. (Now let's see if we can say all this in plain old English.) For the cross-dresser the idea is to bring his or her 'feminine' qualities and desires into a harmonious balance with his or her 'masculine' qualities. The result is a sense of wholeness, or oneness, of being one person, of being both a man and woman-- not two separate identities, but a single identity, a single, complete person.

That to me is a beautiful concept, and a beautiful objective. It is an ideal, but it is an ideal that everyone can achieve. Think of it--peace of mind for all cross-dressers--no searching for an evasive identity, no being lost in a categorical limbo--just being a person, being a man AND a woman in harmony with him AND herself. Beautiful!"

Purpose

The purpose of this book is to help the reader make an easier transition, not to suggest to the reader how far she should go along the path towards total transsexualism. That is a decision for each individual.

In the world of "T"'s, each person is on a different point in a continuum, a spectrum. Think of the continuum as a straight line. The very beginning fetishistic activities are on the left or beginning of the line. The post-operative sex reassignment surgery stage is on the far right end of the line. Each person would place herself at a different point along the continuum. So.

while there is a commonality between our activities, few of us are ever on the same point in the spectrum. Each of us during our lifetime changes points on the continuum, going further one way or the other depending upon a variety of factors.

There is really no particular advantage to "moving on the continuum." Many "T"s seem to feel superior to others if they are further along the road towards sexual reassignment surgery. Yet, if the continuum is used as a measuring stick for accomplishment, too often jealousy at what others have accomplished becomes a motive for deeper change . . . which is not necessarily desirable.

Every person is correct in her own place on the continuum . . . there is no prize for moving towards the surgery, or away from it. The ideal place on the continuum is where we are comfortable with ourselves.

Ours is not to reason why

What you won't find in this book is a lot of psychological jargon or philosophical explanations of why we are what we are. Over the centuries, psychologists and psychiatrists have done their utmost to figure out why individuals feel that they must either dress as woman or actually have sex reassignment surgery in order to achieve mental peace.

Nor will this book be any attempt to help "cure" somebody from "T" tendencies. Despite the best of intentions of professionals of all shapes and sizes, there is no "T" cure. By and large, those with "T" tendencies continue to manifest them, with varying degrees of behavior,

throughout their lives.

Some feel that "T" behavior is compulsive. Compulsion implies that a person has little or no control over her actions, yet if not totally compulsive, "T" behavior is certainly highly conditioned and reinforced by repetition.

Psychologists don't like the word 'compulsive' . . . and feel it is negative. They would prefer the use of such words as "needs" or "strong desires."

This is not a psychological analysis of "T" behavior—simply the author's opinion that a "T" who begins to explore "T"ism, will usually, in one form or another, continue throughout her life.

In this book the pronoun "she" will be used. In almost any stage of development, "T"s prefer to be referred to as of the feminine gender. From both the writer's and the reader's viewpoint, it is much easier to use one gender than to constantly repeat "he/she."

Steps along the way

I have spent a lifetime in preparing for this book, both as a living experience and as a result of having "picked the brains" (and experience) of literally hundreds of "T"s as well as professionals working in one way or another with the "T" Community.

"T"s take a number of similar steps. (Yet certain actions are unique to individuals.) Let's look at the measurable activity shared by "T"s.

A) Dressing under the clothes
  The very first activity of most "T"s, usually in childhood, but oftentimes at an older age, is wearing female

AUTHOR'S NOTE: Throughout this book we will simply use the letter "T." "T" will become all inclusive— a word that covers everyone who is experimenting on the road towards a more feminine gender role, even if only temporarily.

clothing, perhaps even under the male clothing. This might involve wearing underwear—panties, bra, or some other form of female apparel (even hosiery) under male clothes while at work, out in public, or even in the home.

B) Dressing "out of the closet"
Wearing a more complete feminine wardrobe, perhaps even including nightgowns, but dressing at home, remaining at home.

C) Wearing a complete feminine wardrobe and actually going out in public
Even if the public appearances be under some "legitimate" guise such as a Halloween party or similar occasion.

D) Attending events
As part of group activity, support groups, sorority groups or other group activities where there is not necessarily a need to pass as a woman.

E) Attempting to pass as a woman
Actually going out in public, alone or perhaps with a significant other, passing or attempting to pass as a woman.

F) Taking reversible physical steps
Shaving the body, the arms, legs, chest, underarms.

G) Undergoing electrolysis
Generally non-reversible (although if not continued to completion, the beard may grow out after a period of time).

H) Shaving the Adam's apple.
This is a physical step that can be done by a plastic surgeon, is costly, not painful, and removes the last male physical vestige (other than the genitals) that often shows in the genetic male. Many male-to-female transsexuals never need a tracheotomy.

I) Taking hormones
Even with hormone treatment, the physical effects are still reversible via a mastectomy (and by stopping hormonal treatment).

J) Breast implants
Implants are becoming more common for "T"s, especially where hormones, by themselves, do not result in the desired size of breasts. Up to this point on the continuum, every activity is reversible. The next step is not.

K) Having sex reassignment surgery
This is total commitment to surgery. At this point the "T" is no longer a "T"—she is a functioning woman, at least as far as the physical appearance of the genitals is concerned. It is our educated guess that only a minuscule percentage of "T"s ever get to and through this point. (The complete move into society after the sex reassignment operation is not a subject for this book.)

Planning
No matter how far a "T" is going on the continuum, a great deal of planning is necessary.

Let's face it—if your tendency is to be a "T", even a beginning "T"—it doesn't happen automatically. Making a successful transition, no matter how far you wish to go, is not easy at best. Making it without planning or scheduling is impossible.

Becoming a successful "T" is very much like running a business . . . or trying to complete any kind of a project: if you don't know where you're going, you are never going to get there. But making the transition from male to female, even on a temporary basis, can take even more planning or scheduling than businesses or other kinds of projects. Intelligent planning, intelligent scheduling is an absolute necessity for a successful transition.

The transition is made even more difficult because most "T"s, particularly in their early years of experimentation into cross-dressing and its other implications, look at this "hobby" as a temporary thing. Most "T"s do not understand, particularly in the early years, that some form of "T" activity will always be with them, even subconsciously.

Great psychological discomfort can arise from the guilt associated with "T" activities. Family considerations, the feeling that one is alone in her own world, the misunderstanding of society in general about "T"ism, all contribute towards a feeling of unease. Psychologists have a description for it: "cognitive dissonance" or "gender dysphoria."

Part of maturing through the continuum is the gradual understanding that the only way to become a whole person is to face the fact you are a "T"—in one form or another. Accepting the fact, admitting the guilt that you may have accepted because you have let your family, significant other, parents, or society in general, dictate to you what sort of activity "they" find acceptable, can make the transition easier for you to accept.

Yet, looked at positively, experiencing guilt and uneasiness about "T" tendencies can be a motivating factor for planning a more successful transition—or becoming a better cross-dresser (if cross-dressing is your major motivating factor).

To become better at transitioning takes planning—takes careful attention to detail in all of the areas that we cover in the remainder of this book, i.e., body, clothes, make-up, cueing, and in the many other activities involved in the transition.

Professional Help

Certainly those who feel that they are discomforted, especially those who think they may wish to go most or all the way to and through the surgical procedures, should undertake counseling. Physicians who perform the surgery insist on counseling prior to agreeing to the operation. For many "T"s, psychological help has been the one factor that has been most important in the development of "the complete woman."

Every "T", without exception in our experience, has some form of cognitive dissonance. This feeling of unease can express itself in anxiety, depression, tension, guilt, and/or threats to self-esteem. These are normal feelings—they happen to every "T"—and they continue to happen throughout lifetime.

Thus, the "T" must either learn to cope with these feelings or try to leave the "T" world . . . something that is virtually impossible for most. There is not room in this book to go into depth about these human concerns. Suffice it to say that they are natural; everyone has them at one time or another. Every "T", because of her feminine feelings, feelings which usually have not been able to manifest themselves in the everyday world, is more attuned to this unrest than the non-"T" population. Again, outside help and lots of talking—talking—talking, planning—planning—planning, are the only long-term answer for insight and tranquility.

In this book, we continually suggest that when you do look for professional help, you should try to find a therapist, psychologist, or psychiatrist who understands the "T" phenomenon. There is a growing list of professionals who are specializing, or at least understand through practical experience, "T"ism. Using one of these experienced professionals will be more effective in the long run, certainly less expensive because of the removal of the learning curve. You shouldn't have to spend the first six months of counseling teaching the counselor what "T"ism is all about. Throughout this book where we refer to professional help we are always talking about professionals who have worked with other "T"s and who understand the problems and opportunities in this phenomenon.

Regression - purges

In your "T" activities, you will often find yourself going two steps forward and three steps backward. For almost everyone who makes this journey experiences periods of regression. Throughout life, you will seem to get the "T" desires out of your system. Yet, invariably, the feelings, the needs to assume the feminine mode/dress, creep back. If that were not true for you, (if you are a "T") you would not be reading this book.

During these purge time periods, it is not unusual for "T"s to throw away thousands of dollars worth of clothes, makeup, jewelry, and/or other feminine manifestations.

It is also not unusual for the "T" to turn around in a few months and begin again to build her feminine wardrobe.

Many "T"s tell us they have purged over and over again—perhaps five or six times or more, during their lives. In the long run, however, there are no purges that really work. The purges temporarily clear the soul—purges are an attempt to overcome the guilt feelings. "Boy, I'm glad that's out of my system" is a typical purging feeling. Yet little by little, the need to reassume the feminine makes its appearance.

(Perhaps this is a good place to suggest that if you are going to have a purge—only purge as far as taking all of your feminine paraphernalia and getting one of your "T" friends to keep it for you. You can tell them you are purging—they'll certainly understand—and they'll have everything ready for you when you come back out of your guilt-purging activity. It is certainly a lot cheaper in the long run.)

Major measuring points

In your move towards the right-hand side of the continuum, there will be a number of steps that you will take so that you will be able to measure your progress.

We have mentioned the steps of coming out of the closet, i.e., dressing at home, going out in groups, going out alone, mixing in society, being accepted as a woman on a daily basis, living life part-time as a woman, living full-time as a woman, and the physical activities, the body-changing activities that can be taken to expedite each of these moves.

Perhaps the first major move for most "T"s is taking a feminine name. When a name is taken a large psychological step forward is made.

Therapists have a label for the next steps—particularly the steps out into society. "Gender attribution" is the commonly

17

accepted phrase that describes passing in public—having the opposite gender attributed to you because of the way you present yourself. Gender attribution will be covered in a later chapter--it is a vitally important point in the overall "T" activity.

For many, being accepted as a woman is the biggest step of all—perhaps even a greater step than actually going through the reconstructive surgery.

This book, then, is devoted to making gender attribution a reality for those who wish—and assumes that most "T"s reading the book will at one time or another wish to be totally accepted as a woman in society.

Measuring results

How do you measure the results of your "T"ism? How well do you know you're succeeding?

Are you happy enough to simply wear feminine clothing? Do you get a physical satisfaction out of dressing? Is it enough for you to simply wear the clothes? Or do you need to be accepted as a human being of the feminine gender? As an individual woman?

How do you measure the results of each step along the way? Which results are enough? These are just a few of the questions that you will need to ask yourself on a continuing basis.

The answers to those questions will change over the years as you progress in your quest.

The happiest "T"s we know are those who have answered the basic question "Just how much is enough?" We hope that the information in this book will let you determine that point, perhaps even expand your horizons to give you new insights into your journey—so that the desti-

nation of your journey, while it may be further on the spectrum than you originally planned, will still be reachable.

Why this book? A personal note

This book is being written because it feels good for the author to write it.

I wish I had had this book . . . or something like it. . . early on in my life. My transition would have been much easier.

Perhaps, through the help of the IFGE, Outreach Institute, and the other organizations around the world that are in existence to help us share our problems and opportunities, life will be just a little bit easier for those who wish to express, as Dr. Virginia Prince calls it, "the woman within."

The Author's Story

Because I will be referring to my own odyssey throughout this book, it is only fair to give you a thumbnail sketch of where I have been . . . and where I think I am going.

Certainly, I have hit many points on the continuum—having been a "T" from my earliest memory. During the often-mentioned route of wearing my mother's clothing as a child, being totally intrigued with "T"s, having cross-dressing tendencies from earliest childhood and capitalizing on every opportunity to cross, yet being in a society and family that would not tolerate such behavior, I grew up with the usual repressed feelings of guilt and anxiety shared by many "T"s. . . and with which many readers of this book will relate.

A long standing marriage (three decades plus,) the siring of children, the building of a very successful business. . . none of these things were able to erase my "T" desires. Over the years, through constant practice, a great deal of study, plus having the opportunity to travel throughout the world, I put myself in the position of being able to practice "T" activities. I eventually gained the confidence to know that I could extend my "T" activities practically as far as I wished.

At some point in middle age I made the decision that I must be true to myself. I'd reached the "T" stage where I could live and pass as a woman. Yet I was not ready (and may never be) for the final sexual reassignment operation.

After a divorce and reallocation of my financial resources which, luckily, allow me to live as I will and pretty much do what I want without having to earn an additional living, I decided to live my life exactly as I want.

Consequently, I live part of the time on the East Coast of the U.S. as a woman. The other part of my life is spent on the West Coast, as a man. My West Coast life is essentially spent getting financial and other "closure" activities completed. Meanwhile, living part-time as a man gets more and more difficult because I have experienced a complete electrolysis program and have been taking female hormones with increasingly noticeable results.

Where I go from here is still a question mark in my mind . . . but one point is certain. My quest takes me towards the feminine, towards the right-hand side of the spectrum, towards which I am increasingly more and more comfortable.

Chapter 2

Gender Attribution

All "T"s love to pass, or feel that they are passing, as women.

"Passing" may be as simple as riding in a car without someone stopping to shout, "Hey, aren't you a guy?" Or, it may mean living full-time as a woman.

No matter how far they go, all "T"s love to have their gender perceived as female, to rejoice if only for a moment in a sense of themselves as true women.

Four areas of gender attribution are used by "T"s to evaluate passability: the physical body, demeanor (areas of non-verbal response), verbal expression and biography.

We will discuss demeanor and biography. The physical body and verbal expression are discussed elsewhere.

As "T"s progress they develop a biography that allows them to converse intelligently about their past, and a history that helps them to cope with legal and business situations.

In this chapter we will begin our discussion with demeanor.

Demeanor consists of overall appearance and styles of nonverbal communication, including mannerisms. As Anne Bolin says in her book In Search of Eve—Transsexual Rites of Passage:

Much of learning to pass is in the "doing of gender" through interaction with an unknowing audience. However, if the passing performance is marginal, this audience can make a tentative gender assignment. At this point the unknowing audience can become knowing by searching for gender signals and cues to confirm or disconfirm the tentative attribution. In such cases transsexuals realize the equal prominence of all the domains of gender in passing: the physical body, demeanor, verbal expression and biography in contributing to a credible social identity performance.

As experts on the subject agree, including transsexuals who have successfully made the transition, confidence in one's presentation takes time and practice. Transsexuals concur that confidence is an essential part of presenting themselves as natural women, it enhances their ability to pass. In turn, success in passing boosts self-confidence, creating a positive feedback loop.

CUING

Your entree into this positive cycle is the concept of "cueing." You need to incorporate it into your vocabulary, to make it a part of your thinking, to integrate it into your actions.

It is the cueing that you project, the subtle and not-so-subtle signals that you send which will be the deciding factors in how others attribute your gender.

Much of this chapter is devoted to cueing—to stressing how important it is for you to send the right message, to give the right cues. Your demeanor is the key to your cueing.

<u>Being read—whose problem is it?</u>

As a reader of this book and, presumably, a practicing "T" in one form or another, you will want to do your best to display the feminine gender.

After you do your part, the observer also has a "task."

It is the viewer's job to accept you on your terms. In other words, it's "their" problem, not yours.

Only when you realize that the burden of acceptance lies with the viewer can you truly relax in your public appearances.

Kessler and McKenna, in their book <u>Gender</u>, assert that most of the work is done by the perceiver. As a displayer, you can create the initial gender attribution with your public appearance and present talk.

However, after that point, the gender attribution is maintained by virtue of two things: (1) every act of the displayer's is filtered through the initial gender attribution which the perceiver has made; (2) the perceiver holds the natural attitude (e.g., gender is invariant). In short, there is very little that the displayer needs to do once she has provided the initial information, except to maintain the sense of the "naturalness" of her gender. Passing is an on-going practice, but it is practice by both parties. Transsexuals become more "natural" women and less self-consciously transsexuals when they realize that passing is not totally their responsibility. This realisation gets translated into confidence that the other will contribute to making and sustaining the gender attribution and confidence that unless a monumental error is made, the initial gender attribution will not be altered.

People believe what they want to believe and what they are accustomed to believing. What they are accustomed to believing is based on what they see. When they see someone in garb normally associated with a woman, that person <u>is</u> a woman.

This attribution is the viewer's "responsibility." The viewer will believe you are a woman until and unless you do something that drastically alters the original attribution.

An interesting phenomenon that occurs in gender attribution is that once people are convinced of your sex, it is very difficult to convince them otherwise.

Those most experienced in passing tell story after story to confirm the power of the initial gender attribution. Someone accepts them as female, but then a third party misuses pronouns in conversation saying "he" instead of "she" or "his" instead of "hers," even using the male name. Yet once an attribution is made, the perceiver either ignores these slips of the tongue or in other ways assumes that they were simply Freudian slips. At any rate, the attribution did not change.

I have been in numerous situations where after the initial attribution was made, it seemed as though ripping off my clothes was the only way to prove my status as a genetic male (not something I plan to do in the near or distant future!)

Once, during a marathon session trying on clothes, the clerk had ample opportunity, particularly when I was standing in front of her dressed in only a slip, to notice the parts of my body that may not have been "quite right." But because the gender attribution was made there seemed to be no doubt in that clerk's mind that I was the woman I portrayed.

In another instance, I was in a tourist center early one morning reviewing some brochures for an area I was visiting. One of the employees asked me if I would like some cranberry juice. I hadn't talked yet that morning but I turned and answered her. My voice was very low and my throat was scratchy. It must have sounded very much like a man's voice. However, the attribution had already been made and there was absolutely no problem. The remainder of our conversation, once I mustered a more feminine voice, must

have convinced the woman (although certainly unconsciously) that her original attribution was correct.

So what if you are read?

You are going to be read eventually. Count on it.

In fact, you may be read a lot more often than you're aware of.

Somewhere along the way you have to ask yourself those magic two words, "So what?"

What's the worst thing that can happen to you if you're read?

Do you expect the person reading you to run out and call the police? Is that person going to run around screaming, "Look everyone, this woman is really a guy?"

The worst thing that normally happens when you are read is that a person will tell someone they're with about it. They'll look at you—they may smile or laugh, and then they'll go about their business.

They may even say something to you, but how bad can that really be?

Yes, all "T"s shudder when they think of a homophobic pack of males resorting to physical violence when their own masculinity is threatened. It's a horrific vision, but the chances of it happening are remote.

In fact, there are so many people enlightened about "T"ism that even if they do read you, they accept you for your presentation. Although I have mixed emotions about television talk-show presentations on "T"ism (public discussions indirectly threaten our ability to pass by sensitizing the audience), perhaps if more people understand that gender can be socially constructed (i.e., people should be treated as the gender they convey), it might make things easier for us.

Being tall for a woman (although a combination of voice, mannerisms, biography, and dress make me passable), I have been read many times, but then accepted for my presentation as a woman.

I did have one experience which could have been psychologically debilitating. I was driving a car and had become lost in the country. I pulled to the side of the road. A passing policeman noticed that I didn't have any brake lights (the car was a rental) and pulled me over. I showed him my male driver's license and the car rental papers. He checked the license to make sure there were no problems with it in my home state, asked me if I always dressed this way (and of course I replied that I did, that I was a "T" who lived much of the time as a woman), then let me go with a warning to get the lights fixed. Granted, I was lucky he wasn't homophobic but, increasingly, the enlightenment of law enforcement officers as well as the general public makes the realization of your worst fears unlikely, even if you are read.

Bear in mind that in public places most people want to act in a socially acceptable manner. Social pressure will cause them to relate to you according to social norms, even if they discover that you are other than what you appear to be.

You might consider yourself as an actress. In the theater, when an actress gives herself totally to the role she is portraying, no one insists on maintaining or calling attention to her off-stage identity. In fact, many people forget that the actress is not the character she portrays. Indeed, it wouldn't be a bad idea for "T"s to take acting classes.

An excellent article by Angela Gardner in Renaissance News, entitled "How Do You Handle a Read?" concludes with these thoughts:

What does it mean to be read? Sometimes you will be in a public place and you will see someone's lips move in the "It's a man" pattern. What do you do about that? Well, you're most likely not facing any physical danger so what's the big deal? You've just entertained a bored housewife or an accountant whose idea of excitement is a new calculator. Ignore them. Go on about your business and continue to act like a woman. You will stop being a novelty if you just continue to do what you're doing. If they absolutely won't stop staring, try staring back and smile! Most likely they will turn away and try to ignore you.

If you're going to be read at all, the nicest way is to hear someone whisper, "That's a man?" The question in their voice lets you know that although they suspect you're not exactly what you appear to be, your beauty and poise have left large doubts in their mind.

Of course, any read, even the nice, can be a pain. What should you do afterwards? Do you drive home, rip off your wig, wash off your makeup and vow never to indulge in this humiliating behavior again? Of course not. That impulse, like the urge to hide, will get you nowhere. For every read you detect, there are a few you are not aware at all. There are also hundreds of people who see you on your public outings and have no idea that you are anything but what you appear to be. Don't let being read discourage you. No one passes all the time. As long as we only cross the gender line a few times each month, there will always be something masculine about us that, from the right angle, in the right place, to the wrong person, will give us away.

What's important is your attitude. You have as much right to be where you are, dressed as you choose, as anyone else in the place. Ninety percent of the time, if you look and act relaxed, as if you belong there, you will pass. Don't worry about the other ten percent. As long as people who notice don't think it's their duty to rearrange your body parts, then don't let their attention bother you.

Another component of passing that is hard to gauge is the 'getting away with it' factor. Many members of the general public are perceptive enough to notice that there is something wrong with this picture, but they have manners, breeding, style, or they're just too apathetic to care. The point is, don't worry about what they think. Project the image you want to be the best of your ability and enjoy yourself in whatever activities you want to try. Use discretion about where you go and how you dress. Look appropriate and stay relaxed. It's up to you to make your outings into the public arena a fun time that can help you grow personally. Try to remove the anxiety from the experience and ENJOY!

Demeanor - Non-verbal response

Your ability to pass is intimately related to your physical image. Bear in mind that women come in as many varieties as men. If you've applied your make-up reasonably well and if you dress and wear appropriate clothes, chances are that you will pass for female.

As important as the physical side is the emotional or psychological aspect of your presentation. A passable appearance alone is not enough.

If you don't believe you're going to pass, you won't. When that self-confidence is missing, you send out signals—subtle signals indeed but certainly signals—to the rest of the world that something is not quite right.

Particularly at first, it's a good idea to put yourself in situations that you can control, situations where you will have an easier time passing.

You might start by going to places where there is no need for conversation, where you simply walk around and are seen.

They might be places where there are relatively few people or places where everyone is in a hurry where no one sits around staring at and judging passersby.

An initial inclination may be toward shopping centers, where there are hoards of people milling around. Shopping malls can be good and bad. You can easily disappear and blend into the wandering shoppers, but beware of young people. As any "T" who has ever been read by a teenage girl will attest, it is much harder to pass the scrutiny of someone going through her own puberty (who looks to identify with and compare herself against her peers) than it is to pass among adults.

Meeting with other "T"s may be your first opportunity to practice your public presentation. Simply going to and from "T" meetings is a good first experience, one that most of us have used as our introduction moving as a woman into the outside world.

If you don't already belong to a support group of one kind or another, you can find a listing in Tapestry or in your sorority magazine. One phone call to the contact person for that support group will guarantee a warm welcome. If you are very shy, you might wish to attend in your male clothing the first time around. As you become comfortable you'll certainly dress for your second and subsequent visits.

When you visit the clubs or sororities, you'll be nervous at first. We all were, convinced that the entire world knew who we were, that the secret we'd been hiding for years would be revealed, that we'd be read going to and from the club. None of these things happen, of course, but the fear is real the first time out.

In very short order you'll discover with great relief that club members will put you at ease. In fact, you'll probably be a heroine when you tell them that it's your first time out in public. You'll also end up with lots of good cueing tips from your sisters.

Some "T"s enjoy going into gay bars where they feel more comfortable than they might in other public locations. They feel that the acceptance potential is higher in gay bars.

While it is true that there tend to be fewer hassles in a gay bar, over the long run the "T" will find out that she is not really welcome in most gay bars. Generally, gays reject the stereotype of a man wearing women's clothes and acting overly feminine. It is a good idea to phone ahead before you go to a gay bar to ask if you'll be welcome. Don't worry about being harassed, "hit on" or "cruised" at a gay bar. Gay men are looking for other gay men, not for heterosexual men in dresses.

As JoAnn Roberts says in her book

Art and Illusion: "Dressing to pass is work!" JoAnn shows that the "T" must be acutely aware of her appearance and actions, especially during the daytime. Most "T"s begin their adventures in public with heavy make-up and dramatic clothing, usually much too heavy and dramatic for daytime use.

The psychological preparation for appearing in public is different for each person. Some "T"s start with a ride in the car. Others go to a park or public setting where the crowds are not too heavy.

Working up the courage to go to restaurants or other more intimate public places is not easy for a "T." Going with someone, one of the cardinal rules, helps tremendously. The ideal is to go out with another woman, not another "T" but a genetic woman—or with a man. The other person usually diverts attention from or "masks" the "T"—no one looks twice at two people, but one woman, especially alone in a restaurant or bar, often gets the once-over from people of both sexes.

In my early days as a "T," I made an arrangement with another "T." We escorted each other, each of us taking turns in the male/female role. As far as I know, we were never read.

In her book In Search of Eve, Anne Bolin refers to the woman friend as an "age mate system." She explains that as transsexuals near the conclusion of their journey, they hook up with age mates, women friends close to their own age.

In the early stages of passing, "T"s rely on these age mates and others for help and instruction in passing. In my own case I have a number of age mates, women who have become fast girlfriends over a number of years. Not only are we good friends on a woman-to-woman basis, but in public settings they help me to pass. From that standpoint, particularly in my early attempts at passing, these age mates were invaluable.

It's not a great idea, incidentally, to go out in public with other "T"s. Being with other "T"s increases your chances of getting read, particularly if they are neophytes when it comes to appearing in public. As Anne Bolin states, "Passing is best done as a one-woman experience with the aid of a cohort, preferably a genetic girl. Genetic women are recorded as having the manna of a lifetime of experience as women, and consequently are highly valued as cohorts in the passing process." Ms. Bolin cites two reasons for this:

First she can act as a direct tutor, sharing that history of special "for women only" information. Secondly, there is almost an aura of contagious magic about her. It is as if her femininity or femaleness rubs off on her "T" friends by her physical proximity, sharing and doing things together. She also acts as a real life role model in many respects.

Remember, you set the scene, you decide exactly how far to push yourself. These are situations that demand more or less of your presentation as a woman. Experiment until you feel comfortable, learn and grow from your discomfort and never forget that you're in charge, that you position yourself in ways that will determine the expectations for your performance (and acceptance) as a woman.

Carry your real driver's license. If you have reached the transsexual stage, a letter from your psychiatrist or psychologist explaining that you are in transition

might be a good thing to carry. Bear in mind that wearing women's clothes in public is not considered a crime in most jurisdictions, but also remember that degrees of tolerance, particularly among policemen, vary. It is entirely possible that the officer who stops you for a broken tail light will mistake your guise for the disguise of a criminal. You've got a problem if you can't prove who and what you are. Don't take foolish or unnecessary chances—that's the bottom line in the passing game. Having said that, I know that you will push yourself forward as I did. That's what our lives are all about!

Posture

Women are not mannequins. Style is motion, a presentation of yourself in action. The way a woman walks across the room has more to do with the impression she creates than any other facet of her appearance.

Posture and poise are vital to your presentation. How you walk, sit and place your legs and hands paint a moving portrait that can be arrestingly beautiful. Body language colors and defines your appearance far more than the tilt of your nose, the color of your eyes or the weight of your body.

Because they are taller than the average woman, many "T"s have a difficult time with posture.

Here are some suggestions on improving your posture, courtesy of clothier Lane Bryant:

. . . stand with your lower back and shoulders against the wall. Are the outer ends of your shoulders drooping forward? Stretch out the top of your torso. Extend your shoulders backward.

. . . feel your neck. Bring your head

and chin up slightly and place your head flat against the wall. Your eyes should gaze straight ahead.

. . . feel your shoulders. Are they tight? Raised up? Relax them downward. Keep them back. While you do this breathe evenly.

. . . standing with your back and head aligned, shoulders back and relaxed, turn your attention to your legs. Flex your knees, then stand with your weight distributed evenly between them.

. . . put your hands on your hips.

. . . tug your pelvis under and tighten your tummy. Your fanny should be slightly tucked and the small of your back should be elongated.

. . . point your toes directly forward.

Walking with pride will make you feel more attractive almost instantly, and feeling more attractive inspires better posture. So remember, walk across the room with your head up and your back straight. And don't rush.

Women walk more slowly than men, particularly in public places. Watch them carefully as they saunter through the mall and stroll down the street. They take their time, walking slowly but deliberately. Nothing draws attention to a "T" faster than a rapid, hurried walk. Men are expected to walk rapidly, women aren't. Take your time.

The most telltale signals for cueing come from the art of body language. Managing your hands, for example, can be an art in itself. For example, where you place your hands on your hips is a highly visible cueing sign.

Placing your hands on your hips with fingers forward and thumb back adds weight to your hip line. This is especially true if your elbows are held forward creating a silhouette of the body from the front.

To slenderize your hipline, place your hands on your hips with fingers and thumb together, pointing them toward the floor. (This position will slenderize the hips of an overweight person if the hands are placed on the thighs). Placing your hands on the waistline with thumbs forward and fingers back minimizes the waistline. Because the thumbs point downward and towards the centerline of the body at a forty-five degree angle and because the palms press against the waistline, this is the most slenderizing of all the hand-hip positions.

By observing these three rules your hands will always seem lovely no matter what their shape or size:

1) the fingers should be relaxed with uneven spaces between them. This can be achieved by imitating dancers: place the thumb and middle or longest finger together and then slowly open the hand, keeping the middle finger in towards the palm more than the other fingers.

2) the hand should be held at an angle to the wrist, which lends it a relaxed, "at ease" look.

3) the hand should always be seen in profile, either the little finger or the thumb profile.

There are, of course, a couple of "glamour" don'ts to balance the do's: don't hold both hands interlocked at the waist line, it adds weight to your figure. And don't fold your arms to hide your hands, it drags your bustline down, makes your shoulders sag and it adds weight to your waistline.

Your legs give vital cues to your preferred gender. We've mentioned walking, but standing in a feminine position is an art that "T"s should practice.

There are some rules for standing that are age-old and timeless, but still applicable: 1) the feet are placed with one foot forward; 2) the feet form an angle to one another; 3) the front knee is crossed over the back knee; 4) the major portion of the body weight is on the back leg; 5) the body is correctly aligned with the middle of the shoulders over the middle of the hip-bone; 6) the body as a whole presents an asymmetrical or unevenly balanced picture which is pleasing to the eye; 7) the arms form angles to the body.

Other cues that you will master after you've been in the role for a while include activities such as striking a "picture pose." Remember that when a poised woman comes into a room through an open door-way, she pauses for a moment to orient herself. That pause is called the "picture pose" . . . and while it may seem dramatic to you at first, its primary purpose is not glamour but courtesy . . . or in your case, cueing. It also gives others a moment to become aware of your presence.

When you first enter a room, an office, a bus or a business meeting you have one instant during which you command the complete and undivided attention of those around you. In that instant, people evalu-ate you as a potential threat, attraction or nonentity, you either interest them or you don't. In most cases, people form their im-pressions and make vital decisions about a stranger in less time than it takes to blink an eyelash. If you squander that one moment, you will have to work very hard to create an opportunity to make a second impression.

The value of that first free and open moment can't be overstated. What hap-pens during that first "free" moment will most likely affect the remainder of the relationship, if indeed there is a relation-ship. How many times have you heard people say, "When I first met her . . ." or "The first time I saw you I thought . . .?" These are comments made by people who stuck around to check out their first impressions. Think of the countless oth-ers who never bothered.

A gracious woman will take advan-tage of that moment in the doorway to become aware of those present and to appraise the situation. She'll look to see who's in the room, she'll look for a chair that will flatter her height and build. She'll decide exactly how to enter the scene—by wandering through the room and min-gling, moving directly to sit, visiting with the host or hostess or by making a grand and dramatic entrance.

The "picture pose," incidentally, is nothing other than the basic stance we've just described but with the added touch of placing one hand on your hip. You can then place the other hand on the door frame, shoulder high, pointing your fin-gers toward the ceiling. Go ahead! Try it! You'll like it, and so will your audience!

Smiling

We've covered this before and we'll probably cover it again.

Most women smile at other women. In certain situations, they smile at men, too. Obviously, smiling at the wrong man in the wrong place is not high on the list of good cues. Neither is walking around with a frown on your face. It's a negative cue. Most women don't frown or scowl.

A camaraderie exists between women

that does not exist between men. Women look at other women and pay close attention to what they are wearing, the way they are made up, the way they carry themselves and the total image they project.

Women also notice other women with children. Looks between women can signify anything. Generally, when you make eye contact and nod at a woman with children you are telling her you approve of her child, that you probably have a child of your own at home or have had one, and that together you have shared the child-bearing experience.

It's that knowing, understanding, woman-to-woman smile which says "we share secrets" that is one of the best gender cues you can give.

Recently, I was out buying a new pair of glasses. As I tried on the glasses I turned slowly in the revolving seat. There was another woman sitting three or four seats away from me. When I turned towards her, she smiled and mouthed "very nice." That was a woman-to-woman smile—she was approving my new look and although we were total strangers, we shared a moment of intimacy. It was a smile and a comment that most men would not have shared.

You will garner these smiles and approving nods from other women in stores when you are trying on clothes. Women are generally verbal about their opinions on clothes, particularly if they like what you are trying on.

As you improve upon your cueing, you'll find yourself giving compliments to women you meet in social or business situations. You'll be flattered so often that you'll begin to exchange compliments. You'll notice the things that look particu-larly nice on women with whom you come into contact, and you'll say so with a smile. Nothing is a better cue, nothing is a better icebreaker, nothing is more effective for gender attribution than a compliment you give to another woman.

The same cue works with men, although you'll want to remember that men might respond to your flattery in a way that you might not be prepared for. In turn, you might enjoy his attentions, depending on how well you have learned to cope with male flattery as a woman.

Smiles disarm most children. Remember that children are the first to read and the last to make gender attributions. If they see someone large, for example, they often associate "large" with man. Unless you do something to disarm that attribution, you may find yourself hearing the child ask his or her mother, "Momma, why is that lady so big?" or "Mother, is that a man in a lady's dress?" This has happened time and again to "T"s over the years. When you reach the place where you are not read by children, you've taken a major step.

Ladies' rooms

As you go out in public more often, you'll find yourself having to use the Ladies Room.

The easiest advice to give to beginning "T"s about using the Ladies Room is—don't.

Of course that advice is easier to give than take, because nature will call.

In your early days of public appearances, plan trips that allow you to avoid the restroom. By restricting your intake of fluids, you also restrict your output. No great revelation there, but it is a point which many beginning "T"s forget until that embarrassing moment when they have to go into the ladies room no matter what.

Eventually, you'll have to use the ladies room. Here are some cardinal rules for using ladies' rooms:

1) Go in and do your business and get back out. No dawdling to put on make-up. Inevitably, if you stay in the ladies room you'll end up in a conversation, the last thing you want to do.

2) If there is a line to get into the ladies room or a line for the stall inside, go out and wait a while. Come back when there's no line. There's nothing worse than being scrutinized standing in line in the ladies room. Ladies have nothing else to do in line but to look at you, strike up a conversation and check you out. If there's ever a time you're under a microscope, it's in the ladies room. Avoid it.

3) Use a single unit ladies room when possible. That way you can lock the door, take your time, do your thing and leave without anybody bothering you.

4) Sit, don't stand. OK—we know you know that—but why do so many "T"s still stand, still leave the seat up after they're done?

5) If you do meet someone, smile. No conversation is necessary. The other ladies know why you're in the room; just smile, go in and do your thing and leave. If you meet someone coming in or out, smile but keep walking.

6) Wash your hands after going to the toilet. Ladies do . . . so should you.

You won't have any problem in the ladies' room if you play it cool, calm and collected. Don't try to prove anything, and only use it when you have to.

Always remember that the ladies room is one of the few places where you can run into trouble if you <u>are</u> read. No need to tempt fate.

Developing a biography

Gender is historical.

If you want to pass you must give the impression of being and having always been the gender to which you lay claim.

In concrete terms, this involves talking in a way that reveals your history as a woman.

It means that you must conceal your masculine background and create a new past. If you are going to succeed at passing as a woman, long-term, you must re-evaluate and reconstruct your social past.

Another name for this reconstruction is "biographical editing," the development of a personal history that can be used as you get more and more deeply into role performance as a woman.

You started this process when you chose a female name. As you go further on the "T" spectrum, that name will become more a part of you. "T"s seldom change names in the course of their transition into womanhood. Later, many full-time "T"s make the name change legal, sometimes keeping their last name, perhaps using a middle name as a last name or in some cases, picking an altogether different name. (See Chapter 9.)

As you construct your biography you'll soon realize that some things such as your name are relatively easy to change. Other things may be more difficult or even impossible to change (school and medical records, for example).

You have the added problem of remembering what details from your real past you've included in your new history, and which of those have concrete documentation.

Utilizing actual details from the past makes it a lot easier to construct a biography. The very point you're trying to establish—gender attribution—is so powerful that most biographic details can be utilized in either gender. Once someone decides that you're a woman, most items you reveal about your past will be seen as feminine history.

There will be some aspects of your real past that you will never be able to use in your reconstructed biography. Obviously, if you don't plan to live full-time as a woman your history is less critical.

It's a different story when you do decide to pursue your goal full-time, as you develop and extend your social networks to include people who know you <u>only</u> as a woman. Those "T"s who choose instead to live a dual existence are not as eager to get to know others lest their male persona be revealed.

Your efforts to construct a biography will be greatly improved if you talk to other "T"s. "T"s who are further along the road have come to grips with the constructed biography. They have practiced on each other, asked each other questions, and role-played to reach a point where they can handle just about any situation.

Still, much of what it means to be a woman cannot be articulated, cannot be learned by rote. Most "T"s incorporate "facts" into their biographies as they go along. They feel that learning to pass is like learning language as a child, and they give themselves the time and patience needed to accomplish the task.

The trick, if there is an element of magic to passing, seems to be confidence. With experience you learn that others are not quick to sense or alert enough to notice unusual parts of a biography. Bear in mind that most people take you at face value. The key to being accepted by others is your own self-acceptance.

Again, we come back to the word "cueing."

Passing for many of us is an ongoing practice so it becomes important to anticipate difficult questions. We learn to speak in generalities and even to pretend that we don't understand questions that might prompt a revealing answer. We routinize our daily activities and manage ourselves deliberately in ways that prevent our gender from becoming a problem—for other people as well as ourselves.

Kessler and McKenna, in their book <u>Gender</u>, offer an insightful description of gender attribution when they state that:

"(1) gender attributions are based on information whose meaning is socially shared. Not just any information will inform a gender attribution, and certain information (biological and physical) is seen as more important than other information (role behavior).

(2) Once a gender attribution is made, almost anything can be filtered through it and made sense of.

(3) Gender attribution is essentially genital attribution. If you "know" the genital then you know the gender."

<u>Conclusion</u>

Cueing, the process of sending signals that say you are what you purport to be, is difficult to explain.

You know it when you see it, you know it when you've got it.

When you feel comfortable with yourself, others will feel comfortable with you.

Conversely, if you're not comfortable in the feminine role, if you haven't worked at your appearance, your demeanor, your verbal expression and your biography, then the cues you give off will always be misinterpreted.

This is easier said than done. "Spontaneity," the ability to react in your role of choice without thinking, is also easier to talk about than to achieve.

You only get spontaneity, you only become natural, with practice.

You acquire self-confidence by doing it, doing it, doing it.

You begin to build your self-confidence by watching others—imitation is still the most sincere form of flattery.

As you study women, observing their every nuance, you'll find that the more you study them, the better you'll be able to perform in the feminine role.

You'll soon learn that only with verve and courage, only by approaching the problem of passing head-on can you solve it in the real world. I discovered that in situations where I thought I might be read, or in cases that called for attack or retreat, I got the best results by going right at it. For example, during the early days of public outings I was in a shopping center. Four security guards were gathered at the exit, talking. As I walked towards the exit I could have turned an about-face as if I had forgotten something, turned into another store, or made some other move to avoid those guards. I reviewed my options for an instant, recognized a good opportunity to "take it to them," then calmly walked between the guards, excusing myself so I could get to the door. Not only

was I totally accepted, but one of the guards held the door open for me. You can imagine what that did for my morale— it was one more step on the long road towards the acceptance I so earnestly coveted.

Among the most meaningful statements written about cueing are these words from Niela Miller, a therapist serving the "T" community and others.

"My real femininity has nothing to do with ruffles, lipstick or waist measurements.

And I know a few of you who have been able to touch those places in yourself, but very few. A woman is born to carry another human being inside her, and to feed that being from her body. Whether she ever has a child or not, she always has a sense of herself as the potential holder and nurturer of new life. This affects her psyche as does learning to be like mother. She is a relater; to her own inner body (body sensations, dreams, emotions, creative process) and to those around her in wanting to know and listen to their inner beings. Metaphorically, there are perpetual babies grown inside her which she feeds through the revelation (or disclosure) of this inner self to the outside world. Between women this kind of sharing goes on naturally.

Most men in our culture must learn to separate and differentiate themselves from mother, from being like her, being under her influence. The TV has a split; on the one hand, he yearns to be like mother, soft, yielding, attractive, receptive. He overcompensates for these desires by being, often, extremely macho—so that even though, when dressed, he may try to imitate feminine behavior, he cannot quite grasp feminine being as we have described it above. He tends to, in social situations, either maintain this macho behavior: egocentrism, power without love, need to control, lack of intouchness with the inner self—or he goes to the other extreme—passivity, lack of expression, supression of personality—thinking he's being feminine. Well-integrated "T"s learn how to operate more androgynously, ie., appropriate to the situation. In conversation they move back and forth between themselves as the subject under discussion, and the other person as equally interesting; they collaborate more in decision-making processes and support each other's ideas; their physical movements are sometimes exuberant, sometimes graceful—according to their feeling state, not some stereotype about how women move."

One last word of advice. If you're itching to get out and try your wings, go for it. Remember that the worst things that can happen aren't all that bad and that the best things in life are free. If you let yourself go you're guaranteed to have a great deal of fun.

Chapter 3

Clothes Make the Woman

In the minds of most "T"s, clothes really do make the woman. The early stages of "T"ism almost invariably find the practitioner "borrowing" clothes—from a mother, a sister, or some other female member of a household. This transaction is exciting because the "T" can "get away with it"; she is able to wear someone else's feminine clothing without letting that person know.

But at some point every "T" begins to accumulate a wardrobe. Usually this happens when the "T" leaves home. She may go off to college, take an apartment, or in some other way leave the nest. This opportunity to accumulate feminine clothing is a major step in the "T" journey. Owning this feminine clothing is a form of commitment . . . a physical expression of what, for the "T" up to that point, has only been a desire.

In the early stages of transitioning (the change, in whatever degree, from masculine to feminine), collecting cloth-ing—and especially storing it—(particularly storage) is always a problem. It is made even more difficult if there is not total privacy, a luxury few of us are lucky enough to have. Many "T"s have been "discovered" [(and perhaps unconsciously wished for discovery to take place)] when their clothes were found in a remote closet, a storage area, or a suitcase, the most common place of concealment.

There is no magic solution to this storage problem. You will find your own location and will probably worry about being discovered until you have a private place of your own. Leading a "secret" life is difficult and it might make you feel guilty. But remember that you are not alone in hiding your clothing. There are many thousands like you who do the same thing.

Style vs. fashion

Style is different from fashion. Fashions constantly change. From one season to the next, hems go up or down, shoulders are padded or unpadded. On the other hand, style is consistent; it's the foundation upon which you build your "look." First you will need to identify your individual style. Once you've done that, you'll be able to select your clothing to indulge in every "fashion dream" you've ever had.

What is your style? That's something that every "T" at some point has to consider. The style that you choose is probably inside you somewhere, longing to get out.

Close your eyes and envision a woman you've seen dressed beautifully, or an ad you've seen in a magazine, or a look that you've seen in clothing stores. Dream about that look and it will soon crystallize into what will eventually become "your" style. How about a favorite color that you've never worn? Listen to that inner voice; it will probably tell you the right color for your next outfit.

Once you have a feel for your unique style, it's time to put it into practice. Shopping for style takes time. You simply can't put together a harmonious wardrobe from random purchases. You have to build it.

Besides the clothes you wear, style is achieved through impeccable grooming, naturalness, and enjoyment. Your hair must shine, your smile must flash, your nails must be well kept, and your skin must be fresh. You don't adopt a style, you develop it. You'll never be wearing anything that feels like a costume. You'll want to be your most attractive self—not an imitation of someone else. Getting dressed should delight you. It should make you smile. When others see you they should smile, too. So let yourself dress with a touch of pizzazz, use a splash of color, wear an unusual piece of jewelry. Re-

member you can be eye-catching and be yourself.

Your focal point

Just as there's a focal point in every good photograph or painting, there should there be one point of emphasis in every ensemble you create. It's disturbing to the observer if there is none. The more you plan the focal point, the more coordinated your ensemble will be.

Do you want the focal point to be your face? If so, then your earrings, make-up, or a specific blouse might be emphasized. Are your legs your best feature? Then how about wearing a skirt with a slit or heels that are especially attractive?

The focal points can also be used to draw attention away from figure flaws. Layered clothing, for example, can help normalize all figure types. A vest, jacket, sweater, or a scarf can draw interest and give flare and dash; they disguise but at the same time, by completing an outfit, they give it more importance—a pulled-together look that is both chic and casual.

Another important principle of dress is balance. For example, you might balance extra large hips with large tops; wear soft fabrics and lines for large muscles; and emphasize your beautiful hair, nails, jewelry, and make-up if you have an extra large body.

Color consultants

One of the best ways to determine what sort of clothing to buy, particularly the colors and the fabrics, is to get outside help. You might use a professional color consultant.

Because each has her own unique skin tone, it is important to find the colors that best complement this tone to bring out your special beauty. Beautiful women have discovered the power of color to make the world regard them with awe.

An organization called Color Me Beautiful has representatives all across North America who help people plan their wardrobes. These representatives (most of whom are women), analyze each client's coloring, give her a packet of fabric swatches in her color palette, and teach her how to use them as a guide for shopping and looking beautiful. Color Me Beautiful consultants help with individual make-up, hair, and even personality and style.

The Color Me Beautiful concept links people to the four seasons. Each season has its own harmonious colors. A person's genes give her a type of coloring that is complemented by one of these seasonal palettes. Once the Color Me Beautiful professional has worked with her to discover her seasonal look, she'll learn what colors make her fabulous all the time; she'll move on to learn exactly what make-up and hair tones are perfect for her. With this professional help, she will have the ability to make the right fashion choices for herself to project her best image. Actually "It's the power," as the Color Me Beautiful people say, "to be beautiful on the outside, to feel beautiful on the inside."

To find the Color Me Beautiful consultant nearest you, call 1-800-533-5503. If you live in Virginia, call 1-703-471-6400 or you can write to Carole Jackson, P. O. Box 401, Chantilly, Virginia, 22021.

But if you can't afford professional help to plan your wardrobe, there are some basic tenets you need to know to make yourself more beautiful.

You'll need to know the kinds of colors, patterns, and dress lengths to buy that fit well with your body structure:

1. Light colors will make you look larger, dark colors make you look smaller.

2. Vertical and horizontal lines and large, spaced-out print patterns are enlarging; but small, continuous print patterns have the opposite effect.

3. A light top and a darker bottom will improve a bottom-heavy woman's appearance and a dark top will help the look of a top-heavy or large-shouldered woman.

4. A longer jacket will reduce the appearance of height in a tall figure, and a short jacket will create the illusion of height in a short figure.

5. Attract interest to the bosom with the addition of detail and use detail to direct interest to the hipline (in this concept, detail is defined as lace, striping, pleats, anything other than simple, plain cloth).

Buying clothes

The first major hurdle in buying feminine clothing is one that every genetic male faces—the embarrassment of the purchase.

Almost every "T" has been frightened buying women's clothing, particularly lingerie. The only solution to overcoming this fear is experience. You'll simply have to do it again and again to gain confidence and to accept the fact that there's nothing wrong with buying feminine clothing.

One of the major transition points for many "T"s involves garnering enough nerve to go into a ladies' store, dressed as a proper lady, picking out clothes, trying them on, buying them, or putting them back on the rack. If you are to this point in your transition, you will know it.

Decide why you're going shopping

Did you ever go shopping only to find out that you really didn't know what you were looking for, and you wandered aimlessly from rack to rack, getting more and more frustrated every minute? There's a cure for this "disease":

Decide before you leave the house if you're going to browse, not buy. You won't be disappointed if you come home empty-handed. If you do plan to buy, decide exactly what you're going to want. Give yourself a specific assignment. Then, when you get to the store, go directly to the department that has the item you need. Focus your attention on obtaining that item. Only after you've accomplished your task should you look around and see what else you might like to buy. You'll feel satisfied that the shopping trip was time spent well.

Rely on the salespeople. Normally they're eager and ready to help you. Obviously, this is not always true, but recently retail establishments seem intent on providing satisfying customer services.

Remember, salespeople are there to make sales. We have never heard of a case where a salesperson would not sell clothing to a "T" because the salesperson knew it was for the "T" herself. Many salespeople work on commission, but even those who don't are not going to question who is going to wear the clothing.

The worst that can happen is that you are asked, "Does the lady for whom you're buying this like this color, this size, or this style?" Because you are "the lady" you can answer it properly with a "Yes" or "No," or whatever comments you may have about the clothing. Many "T"s,

however, tend to explain too much. They feel so embarrassed about buying feminine clothing for their "wives" that they go into too much of an explanation—making themselves even more suspect. Again, remember that the salesperson really doesn't care. Chances are she or he simply wants to sell clothes, get your money, and go on to the next customer.

When I formerly went to buy women's clothes dressed as a male, I did not hesitate to tell the salesperson that I was buying the clothes for myself. I didn't necessarily say that I was a "T", although they may assume such, but I might have said that I was going to a party or doing a show. When I went back to the same store, I found that the salesperson understood that I was buying for myself. This type of salesperson didn't mind talking to my about my needs.

In fact I met one of my best girlfriends when I was buying clothes for myself. At first she thought I was buying clothes for my wife. After three or four visits to the store I finally told her that I was buying the clothes for myself. This broke the ice and she was very friendly. She wanted to know more about my "T"ism and we eventually became good male and female friends, and then, as girlfriends, as I furthered my own transition.

You may find that you want to browse a bit, try on a few things, and not buy. But women often get into an extended session of trying on clothes and realize it's not going well. They automatically begin to look through the items they've tried on to see which would be the least odious token purchase.

You do not need to waste your money that way. It isn't your fault that the size that you're looking for isn't available and that the store's shelves are inadequately stocked. Simply thank the clerk. If she's been helpful, tell her so; say you'll be back again and then leave. Shopping can become a more pleasant experience when you realize that sales personnel are just as human and just as insecure as the rest of us. They don't really mean to be nasty, and they probably won't be unless you allow it. You'll be very welcome when you go back into the store.

There are times, however, when you purchase something that you think you really like. When you get home, you find that the outfit doesn't fit as well as you had thought. What you should do then is return the clothing. Remember, women often return clothes and exchange them for a different size or get credit at the store for another purchase. There is absolutely nothing wrong with this. In fact, women sometimes take clothes home, wear them to a function, and then return them and get credit. This is not a move we would advocate, but it proves how far some women go to take advantage of the return policies of stores. Such policies should be kept in mind by those "T"s who shop as males. They cannot try clothes on in stores, and because the clothes-buying forays are so embarrassing to them, they hesitate to return ill-fitting garments.

Going shopping
Shopping is fun—if you let it be. But to have fun, you'll need to start with a positive attitude. Compliment yourself. Don't worry over imagined flaws. Don't start out feeling scruffy or not-pulled-together.

Take time to get dressed up to go shopping. Wear your favorite, most flattering comfortable outfit. Wear under-

wear, foundations, and hosiery that make you look and feel good. Make sure your hair and make-up are flattering. Wear shoes that will look good with the clothes you're going to try on.

The dressing room
The first time I went into a store and heard one of the clerks say, "Ma'am, would you like to try that dress on?" I knew that I had arrived at one of the turning points in my "T" journey. I knew that gender attribution was complete; she saw me as a woman. After that, I never feared going into a store and trying on clothes.

Stores usually have a rule about the number of garments you can take into the dressing rooms. Follow their policies; the last thing you want is to be stopped because you have too many garments over your arm. Moreover, you don't want to be suspected of shoplifting.

You may want to remember these tips when you are using dressing or fitting rooms:

1)Take in a complete outfit; don't try on one piece at a time. If you're shopping for a feminine/silky blouse, you'll never know how flattering it is if you try it on with your jeans. Bring in a beautiful flowing skirt so you can see how it will look as an entire outfit.

2)When you get dressed, don't stand at the mirror. Turn your back to it until you have on the entire outfit. Then turn and smile.

3)Step as far back from the mirror as possible to get a good picture of how the clothes work together and how they fit you.

4)Move around, do a dance step, twirl or walk. Clothes—and people—are made to move! Go out and ask the salespeople for their advice and feedback. They may suggest changing the color of a top or trying a skirt of a different style. Experiment, and let them cheer you on.

5)It is important that you wear the newly tried-on article out into the store where you can see your movement in the full-length mirrors. Chances are a salesperson will come up to you and give you her advice. That advice will be especially helpful if you created a rapport with her, told her specifically what you were looking for, and had her help you pick out the garment.

Remember, feel free to ask lots of questions. You don't have to buy something you're not really in love with; nobody is forcing you to make the purchase. You have your right of choice. Love what you're going to buy, make sure it looks good on you, get the opinions of others who will tell you what they think and then . . . go for it!

Additional tips

If you're trying on an important garment (defined as a more expensive garment or one that will be an essential part or base part to your wardrobe) you should put the whole look together in front of the mirror. You can fix and fuss just as if you were getting dressed at home in order to see if the garment is really for you. Relax and take your time; that's what a dressing room is for. Then look at yourself objectively and try to imagine an impression you would make walking into a room wearing that garment.

Try sitting down in a dress, a skirt, or pants. Scrunch the fabric in your hand to see if it wrinkles too easily. Bend over, reach out, squat. Does the garment do all the things you'll want it to do when you're

actually wearing it? Can you move in it? Is the armhole of the garment set where your armsocket is?

Before making a final decision, be sure to check the labels to see what kind of cleaning or washing care is needed. Are you willing to do what is necessary? Also, take into account possible problems with shrinkage.

Just the facts, ma'am

You may be new at shopping for women's clothing but you probably know more than you think. Clothing is clothing. . . whether it be women's or men's. For example, the better the clothing (usually the more money you pay for it) the longer it will last and the better it will look.

The natural inclination of a beginning "T" is to buy the least expensive clothing possible, even clothing bought at the Salvation Army or thrift stores. She is not alone. Everyone loves a good bargain, even women who have been shopping all their lives and women for whom money is no object.

But why do so many "T"s buy inexpensive clothes? Perhaps part of the thrill is in the shopping . . . it is "kicks" to be able to go in stores and actually discourse with the clerks about various garments. As you go through your transition, however, you will find that instead of buying so many clothes, you will begin to buy fewer and better clothing that you can wear again and again, perhaps with different acessories. You will gravitate towards the clothes that are comfortable and look best on you, wearing them many times as you gain confidence in your appearance and are accepted more readily. It is amazing how passing as a woman in a certain dress, suit, skirt and blouse, or other outfit will often bring you back to that outfit. This behavior will seem familiar to you as you probably wear a few favorite outfits when you dress as a male.

A cardinal rule of thumb, particularly if budgets are limited, is to buy the basics. When buying fashion items, start with one versatile piece such as a sweater or a jacket. You can combine that piece with many different outfits and vary your accessories to make bolder fashion statements. A skirt, neutral in color (perhaps black), can go with any kind of top. One or two dresses, attractive accessories, and two or three blouses, will provide you with enough clothing to wear in practically any season. The key words here are "good" and "basic."

Many "T"s go a little wild when they begin to buy feminine clothing. They buy anything in sight, and the frillier the better. It is best, however, to curb your natural appetite and to buy practical clothing. This may be difficult to do, but bear in mind that the better the clothing you buy, the longer it will last, the better it will fit, and the more you will like it.

If money is a problem, try to mix one expensive item with something of lesser quality. Some fashion experts suggest that you wear the expensive item near your face, i.e., put the showpiece on top. A well-made blouse or jacket will instantly enhance the impression you make, whereas an inexpensive skirt that fits well is fine because people don't study it when you are seated or moving. Don't let a salesperson talk you into getting a garment that doesn't fit. Certainly most stores have alteration departments, but alterations for women's clothing are expensive; they're not free like they are in men's

stores. Moreover, it is almost impossible to alter the shoulders of a coat, dress or suit. (The shoulders should come out even with the outside of the shoulder bone, no matter what the clerk says.)

As you get more proficient at buying clothes, you will recognize that certain styles of sleeves, for example, will work better on you than other styles. Or you will find that you might be able to wear a size 16 in a shirtwaist dress and a 12 in an A-line dress. Different cuts in women's clothes mean that sizes aren't as standard as they are in men's clothes. You will have to find this out for yourself. Don't be surprised when the size 14 that looks so good on the rack and in the ad in the paper, is at least two or three sizes too small when you get it home.

You may also experience the opposite scenario which is very exciting. I distinctly remember the time when one of my woman friends who understands clothing much better than I, accompanied me to a coat store. I looked at scores of winter coats before I tried on a size 14. Because my normal size is 20-22, I almost refused to put on the coat. When I slipped my arms through the sleeves, however, I knew immediately it was the coat for me. My friend had noticed the cut of the coat, knew that it was cut large, and knew that it would fit my shoulders. The sleeves had to be let out, but the rest of the coat fit perfectly. I wouldn't have tried on this coat—my best piece of winter clothing—if she had not understood that different cuts of clothing fit different bodies differently.

Back to the basics

Let's look at some basic kinds of clothing. I do not claim to be an expert about high fashion, but only hope to explain different types of clothing from a "T"'s standpoint. This information will help you make clothing decisions that do not involve knowing the "in" fashions.

Dresses: Many "T"s, believing that their mothers dressed in the height of femininity, buy dresses that they think their mothers would wear. However, the average woman today does not dress the way her mother does or did.

Dress advertisements, even dresses on racks in stores, look alluring. You may please the advertisers and imagine yourself in one of these dresses, but chances are you do not have a model's body (unless you're a very, very lucky "T").

So, what kind of dress looks good on you? Only you or some professional advisor might know best. What kind of dress should you buy? The most practical tip is to look and see what other women are wearing. That sounds simplistic, yet it is really the only answer. It's simple enough to see the styles; look at the women in your office, in your shop, at home, out shopping, out for the evening.

You will learn not to buy anything drastic. Most "T"s begin their journey by buying their dresses too short. They feel that shorter dresses are for younger girls, and if they wear shorter dresses they will look younger. But shorter skirts show legs that usually aren't as attractive as they might be on, say, an eighteen-year-old lady. These "T"s soon discover that the higher the hemline, the older they look. Longer dresses can cover a multitude of sins on the legs. But even if you have the best legs in the world, your dresses, particularly if you're going to wear them on the street or in everyday situations, should probably have a length somewhere below

the knee and above the calf. Longer dresses and skirts are also very fashionable, and as your wardrobe builds you will find yourself having a few dresses that will have hemlines almost to the ankle. Often a "T" finds that when she is brave enough to wear longer dresses, and even jeans or pants, she doesn't need to look frilly in order to pass. Generally, the simpler the look of the dress—not too low cut, not too much lace or other frills—the more natural you will appear.

Skirts, sweaters, blouses:
The woman on the street wears skirts and sweaters or skirts and blouses, pants and sweaters or pants and blouses. In her everyday life, she may occasionally wear dresses; certainly she does so for a dress-up affair. But essentially she dresses down for her everyday wear. She is not a fashion plate and does not go shopping to the store, or run her daily life, in high heels and high fashion.

Yet for "T"s, particularly beginning "T"s, dressing down is very difficult. Only the most sophisticated "T"s are able to dress down. The transition is relatively complete when she is willing to put on jeans, a sweatshirt and a little make-up, pull back her hair, and go about her business.

At first, most "T"s buy long-sleeved shirts, blouses, sweaters, and dresses. The long sleeves do cover up unsightly arm hair, but if there is little or no hair problem, long sleeves really don't accomplish anything. The average woman, on the other hand, pushes her sleeves up or wears short sleeves. She seldom wears sweater sleeves over her wrists. She likes to show off her thin wrists or her jewelry.

Most beginning "T"s also wear high-necked blouses, sweaters, and dresses. Such clothing is fine, but as the "T"s become accomplished their necklines fall to where they look more natural. Obviously the chest hair and the tracheal bump—the Adam's apple—must be considered and perhaps covered up. Beginning "T"s also wear blouses and sweaters that are too tight for them so that they can emphasize the size of their breasts. In this day and age, women tend <u>not</u> to emphasize their breast size. (Although it will be mentioned again, this is as good a time as any to bring up the fact that oversized breasts make a less than acceptable feminine appearance. The object of most "T"s is to call attention away from themselves, not to have people stare at the size of their breasts or the shape of their legs if the skirt is too short.) It's a natural tendency to believe that tighter clothes make one look smaller—except for the breasts—but actually the opposite is true. The more loose fitting the blouse or the sweater, the more comfortable the person appears. Loose-fitting clothing minimizes size. And don't forget bulky sweaters—the kind you can practically swim in. Not only are these always fashionable, but they can hide unflattering body shapes. Button-up sweaters thrown over the shoulders, also minimize the upper torso.

Sweaters over sweaters are very attractive, particularly sweaters on sweaters of the same color. Cashmere is a favorite of "T"s, but if you can only afford one sweater, try to make it a good one if at all possible. Also, pushing up the sweater sleeves establishes a very feminine look. Remember, too, that sweaters should be bloused from the waist to soften the waistline.

Lovely lingerie:

Beginning "T"s love to buy lingerie, but they quickly find that the frilly, fancy, lacy undies, which look good on models, are not very practical in the real world. Early on, they almost invariably succumb to buying garter belts, long-line corsets and bras, and very restrictive lingerie. Although they enjoy the sensual feeling that this lingerie brings (and the security it gives to know that their genitals are being hidden), it soon becomes obvious that the more comfortable the undergarments, the more comfortable the "T" feels in her daily activities.

Stockings:

The best all-around color for stockings is one that is a shade darker than your natural skin color. The stocking texture should go with the mood of your shoe—a rough-textured country stocking with a low-heeled walking loafer and a sheerer stocking as your heel gets higher and the shoe becomes delicate.

It's nice to be cute; maybe you can dress up for your favorite girlfriend (or boyfriend) or your fellow "T"s. But on a practical basis, day in and day out, nothing beats pantyhose. Pantyhose also cover a multitude of sins, including too much hair. A pair of supphose under a pair of pantyhose covers up practically any hair, particularly helpful for those "T"s who find they cannot shave their legs. Pantyhose can last forever (although don't tell that to your favorite girlfriend who invariably runs her hosiery when she's down to her last pair and is just ready for a hot date). If you buy reasonably priced ones, keep them washed and properly folded. In fact, <u>all</u> undergarments need to be washed after wearing and then stored in a rolled up or folded manner. A small amount of Woolite in a basin of cold water will do wonders. Simply let the hose or garments soak for a few minutes, rinse them out, blot them in a towel, hang them up, and note how they dry in a few hours. The way "T"s treat their underwear, incidentally, is often an indicator of the way they run their lives. No kidding!

Lingerie:

Your underwear should be the same color even though nobody will notice but you. But what if you are hit by a car and taken to the hospital? Didn't your mother always tell you that your underwear should match and be clean?

Seriously, white bras don't go with black slips—or vice versa. Wrong-colored bras and slips <u>always</u> show through blouses. Note the emphasis on "always." Light blouses call for light underwear and dark blouses or dresses call for dark underwear. That sounds simplistic, but it's one important point a lot of "T"s don't notice.

If there is a cardinal rule about lingerie, it involves one word: simplicity. The more practical your underwear, the more comfortable you will be. Granted, there are times when you want to feel more feminine, more sexy, more frilly. Naturally you will have underwear for every occasion; we all do. But by and large, the simpler the lingerie, the longer it will last, the more comfortable you will be, and the more you will be dressed like all other women.

Shoes:

Shoes used to be a problem for many "T"s, but no longer. Stores that publish catalogs solve the needs of many "T"s, particularly "T"s with larger feet. One of the most reputable "catalog stores" is Tall-Gals Shoes in Norwell, Massachusetts (72 Accord Park, Norwell, 02062). But you need not buy good shoes from a catalog; you can go into a store and buy shoes. Follow the general clothing tips outlined above.

Granted, it is difficult to try on women's shoes if you are dressed as a male. Although we've seen it done a few times, it is awkward, at best. To avoid this scenario, take the shoes home, try them on, and return them if they don't fit. People often buy shoes for their family or friends, then return them. Shoe store operators are used to shoes being returned unworn. So don't hesitate to take them back if you aren't happy with them. Get shoes that feel good and, of course, look good.

"T"s tend to buy high-heeled shoes, especially very high ones. In the real world, however, few women walk for any appreciable distance in high heels. Sure, it is fun to wear high heels occasionally to see how they can narrow the calf, making it look more feminine. But it is not fun to walk in high heels for many hours at a stretch, as any woman will tell you, and any "T" will find out.

Walk with the toes pointed straight ahead. (Men tend to point their toes outward.) If you want to practice your "feminine walk," you should buy and wear a pair of heels. Small heels are in. They are wonderful because when you wear them, you feel you are in high heels. Even if you are tall, there is no reason to avoid wearing a heel, particularly a small one. The little bit of height that the heel adds will not call additional attention to you. But what the heel can do for the calf, for your general appearance, and for your psyche, can be very feminizing.

Buying very simple shoes is usually a good idea and a welcome addition to any basic wardrobe. Black flats or heels, or other shoes of a neutral shade will go with almost any outfit. Ornate shoes are not a part of women's everyday work or shopping clothing. You may be tempted to buy fancy shoes, but in the long run, as you move towards the complete transition, you will gravitate towards simpler shoe wear.

Owning a pair of women's walking or jogging shoes is also a good idea. They are not much different from men's jogging shoes except for their more feminine appearance. When you are able to wear jogging shoes and the short white socks that go with them, you will know you have reached another plateau in your "T" journey.

If you feel that your feet are too wide and you wish to lessen the width, buy shoes that have vertical and diagonal stitching, are low cut at the instep, and have a moderately rounded toe. If you would like to lessen the lengthy look of your foot, buy shoes that have a bow or narrow strap across the instep, a rounded vamp, and a rounded toe. If you wish to hide your feet, avoid fancy, flimsy footwear, platform shoes, ankle straps, and loud colors.

<u>Overcoats, gloves, et al.:</u>

Overcoats can also hide a multitude of sins.

Generally the more you pay for an overcoat or a coat of any kind, the better you will look. Granted, you may not be able to afford the expense, but if you are going to splurge on anything, splurge on a coat. You may be outdoors in cold or even fall weather . . . and you'll want to look feel your best.

Coat sizes can be tricky; you will probably have to try on a number of coats before you find the one you like. But remember stores' return policies. You can take coats home, try them on, bring them back, and exchange them. This could get awkward because you may need to buy coats on sale. (In fact, you may buy a lot of clothes on sale.) Sales are often final transactions; you cannot take your item home and try it on.

A good set of gloves is also important . . . obvious to those who live in cold climates. But finding gloves that fit—and gloves that do not call attention to the hand—can be difficult.

Because most "T"s like to minimize the size of their hands, the more slimming the glove the better. Leather gloves generally are slimming, and black ones do the best job. Yet, in very cold climes, women wear mittens and larger gloves to keep warm. This is a choice many "T"s will have to make; do they want to be fashionable or opt for comfort?

If you have a hard time finding gloves that fit, look for Isotoners. This brand features men and women's gloves that look alike. You might also shop for gloves in ski shops; ski gloves and mittens are unisex.

Scarves can go a long way towards feminizing a not-so- feminine look. They can add a dimension that is very attractive. (I have received more compliments on scarves I have worn than on any other piece of clothing.)

Scarves are also popular, at least at the time this book goes to print. More and more women are wearing scarves around

44

the coat or under the coat and across the bosom area. The only time women wear scarves on their heads is if it is raining or snowing. Scarves these days seem to be for decoration. Tying or draping scarves is an art in itself. Observe models, browse through Vogue and other fashion magazines, and look at women on the streets for scarve-tying and wearing ideas.

Hats:

Some "T"s can wear hats and some can't. If you can wear them, enjoy them. They provide a good way to create an instant image. Put one on, and you have a totally new look; take it off, and you have changed again!

The right hat seems to look better and better as it becomes more and more "you." Remember that hats tend to make quite a strong statement; so if you plan to wear hats consistently, people will think of you with a hat on. Hats are ultra, ultra feminine and a real plus to your appearance.

Handbags:

Nothing makes a "T", or any large woman, look more grotesque than a very small purse. (Not all "T"s are large, but "T"s generally have larger frames than other women.) Relatively large purses—at least large enough to be utilitarian and to look natural—should be carried.

You will want to be able to carry everything that you will need in your daily activities.

It is embarrassing to have to dig into a purse to find keys, a billfold, or make-up. Organized women have a place in their purses for everything.

Shoulder bags are popular and practical. They are easier to carry than heavy shopping bags. Clutch bags are not very appropriate for most "T"s except if they are used as evening wear. They are usually smaller than a bag a "T" should carry and are certainly more awkward to deal with during the course of a normal day.

If you can have only a few handbags, start with these four: a medium-large, luggage-leather shoulder bag for the day; a luggage-leather, medium-size clutch bag; a burgundy, medium-size pouch clutch; and a black-fabric evening clutch. Your bags should match the color of your shoes and should be a classy, all-purpose color. The match doesn't have to be perfect, but the color family should be the same. The eye will complete the optical illusion of the nearly matching colors because it wants the two items to go together. You can wear a textured bag such as straw with shoes of any color. In the spring and summer, it is acceptable to carry a patent-leather bag with leather shoes or vice versa. As long as they are the same color, they both don't have to be patent leather. Leather with suede is also permissible if they are in the same color family. Plastic is plastic—in whatever form it comes. All of us at one time or another carried plastic bags of some kind. But bear in mind the more expensive looking a purse, the more expensive looking the carrier of the purse will be.

So the general rule for all clothing certainly applies to handbags, too. The better the bag the classier the individual looks. The bag is often the first thing that other women notice. A sloppy or worn bag, particularly a cheap one, gives the user a bad image, as any woman who knows about feminine dress will tell you.

Perfume:

Your scent might be called a highly evocative accessory. You probably should not change scents as often as you change your outfit.

Scents seem to be a personal signature. Choosing your own scent seems to be a way of establishing your own individuality. Sometimes it is a nice idea, however, to change to a new perfume when a chapter in your life changes. Chances are you will experiment with a lot of different perfumes. It does not hurt to ask others how they react to the perfumes you are wearing.

Integrating new clothing:

Immediately after making a new purchase, while you are still excited about it, integrate it into your wardrobe. Spend some time in front of the mirror. Mix and match it with your other clothing to make as many new and improved outfits as you can. Have on your make-up, your hair combed, and wear the right shoes. Check your accessories for those that suit the various combinations, and make a list of everything else that you might need.

Buy that new or different fashion look, take it home, and practice it. Sit, stand, walk. Coordinate the garment with your body. Integrate it with your own mannerisms—learn to move with it. You will find that you will like the garment a lot more if you become familiar with it before you wear it out in public for the first time.

Chapter 4

Make-up

Professional help

Make-up is one area where professional help is available . . . and always useful.

There are quite a number of services now advertised in magazines such as Tapestry and other "T" publications. Make-up artists advertising in those publications are normally reputable people who are used to dealing with "T" problems, including beard shadows.

Even after you find a professional make-up person to help you pick out the proper make-up and teach you to apply it, you might find that you still want to experiment.

Prior to my living part time as a woman, I found it simple enough to go into make-up counters and department stores (in my experimentation days) and tell them that I was an actor or doing some video work and asking them what kind of base make-up, as well as foundation went with the color of my skin. I received some terrific advice from professional make-up artists . . . advice on make-up I am still using today.

As with clothing salespeople, make-up professionals are there to sell make-up. They're happy to help you—they're not there to ask you reasons why you need the make-up help.

Make-up clinics are often held at Fantasy Fair, group weekends, or other types of "T" get-togethers. The sharing that goes at these functions is heart-warming. Almost invariably somebody there will be more advanced in the use of make-up than you . . . and because of the sharing feelings engendered at these meetings, she'll be happy to help you with your make-up problems. It is a rare "T" who won't share her make-up ideas with her sisters.

Genetic women have been putting on make-up from the time they were ten or twelve years old. This means that they have been practicing—practicing—practicing. Granted many of them never got really good at it—but at least they are more familiar in methods of using make-up than are most "T"s.

To perfect anything in life mistakes must be made. Those who have spent their entire lives living as girls/ women, have had plenty of criticism from their friends and relatives. They aren't afraid to ask—and neither should you be afraid to get help from those who care about you.

The better you get, the more experienced you are at make-up, the less make-up you will use. Less is generally better. The ideal situation is have no one notice that you are wearing any make-up at all. In fact, as we've said before, being able to wear no make-up is a sign of having "arrived" for experienced "T"s.

As you get more adept it takes less and less time to put on make-up. Those of you who have watched a mother or a wife put on her make-up . . . or those of you who have waited for them seemingly interminably, know that make-up times vary for everyone. At first, most "T"s take forty-five minutes to an hour, even longer, to do their make-up. It is usually the eyes that take the bulk of the time.

But as one gets more proficient, a full make-up job can take as little as fifteen or twenty minutes, sometimes even less. While there is usually no particular need to hurry the situation (planning ahead is usually the sign of a relaxed "T") it is nice to know that, in case of emergency, make-up can go on in a very short period of time. There is a certain aura of competence that you gain in putting on make-up . . . and that spills over to your personality when you realize that it is not the time taken to put on make-up that counts

The Beard

Men have beards. Women don't.

Male facial features, generally, are more pronounced than genetic female features. So it is vitally important for the progressing "T" to learn to use make-up properly.

Almost every "T", in her beginning experimentation, uses a great deal of make-up, apparently assuming that the more make-up used, the more defects will be covered.

As "T"s progress, they generally use less and less make-up. In fact, many post-operative transsexuals use little if any make-up, even including lipstick.

Hopefully, this chapter will convince you that there is the proper amount of make-up for you—not too much nor too little—that will help you look as close to the image you are trying to portray as you wish.

Let's start with the obvious—the beard.

Shaving away the shadow

Some of us have a deep five o'clock shadow—a thick beard that, despite the best of intentions and all of our efforts, grows, and keeps on growing.

Luckily, most beards can be removed by diligent shaving. At least whiskers can be removed for a few hours at a time. But as any "T" with a natural five o'clock shadow will tell you, removing the hair long enough to be _en femme_ for a number of hours is a task often beyond the best of intentions.

Electric razors simply don't shave close enough. It seems that shaving with a blade is the only solution that allows deep enough beard removal, five o'clock shadow type removal—so that one can apply proper make-up and remain covered initially and throughout the day, or evening.

"T"s say "I shave very close." This doesn't necessarily mean that they put more pressure on the razor in order to get closer. "Shaving close" for most "T"s consists of shaving twice--shaving the first time, then lathering and shaving again— shaving over the same places.

It also helps to shave against the grain—something that most men don't do in a regular day's shaving. Dermatologists say that repeated shaving against the way the hair is growing, while it does cut the hair off closer to the skin, also may damage the epidermis.

Electrolysis is one long-term answer . . . but it's also an expensive, time-consuming, and painful experience. No one has come up with any shortcuts to electrolysis. So if you read articles or other information about "painless removal of the beard" or "quick beard removal," take those articles with a grain of salt.

Should you desire to undergo electrolysis, remember that the procedure for the average male, for complete beard removal, takes a minimum of one hundred hours . . . and many "T"s I know have spent as much as four or five hundred hours undergoing the procedure.

Experimentation with make-up on the shadow created by a beard—even a removed (by shaving) beard is a "T" fact of life. Successful cover-up is especially important on the whiskers above the lip and on the chin.

Many "T"s, indeed many women, find that a base coat of a cover-up type of make-up underneath a foundation make-up, will keep the beard or the shadow generated by a beard beginning to grow

out, disguised for a period of six to eight hours.

There are a number of make-up products used to cover the beard . . . and there are probably as many different forms of doing this as there are "T"s who have tried it. Experimentation obviously is the answer . . . but my suggestion is to begin with an "Erase" type product . . . one designed to cover blemishes. Once that cover is applied (and some "T"s, incidentally, use a white make-up, even a clown white make-up to cover the beard), the foundation make-up will disguise the cover-up base.

Get additional make-up ideas from other "T"s. Eventually you will develop your own answer on beard cover-up, enhancing the tips that you get with a great deal of experimentation. Trial and error is the only final answer.

You should do make up in all sorts of light—daylight, artificial light, office light . . . and in all sorts of situations.

Ask a friend who will tell you the truth whether or not your five o'clock shadow or your beard shows through. You will eventually find a cover-up that works for you, always bearing in mind that simply adding more make-up is not a long-term answer.

More information on the beard, and the electrolysis process, is contained in Chapter 5.

Make-up tips

Wearing make-up should not look as if you are wearing a mask.

Remember that the major difference between the physical appearance of many genetic males and females is the prominence of features—nose, cheekbones, heavy jaws, eyes.

49

Learning how to minimize the larger features is an art—but one that's relatively easy to do when the basics are understood.

For example, highlighting the cheekbones is a relatively simple process, if done properly, and can radically change the look of a face. Practice is the only answer, but to determine how to highlight the cheekbones, you might try this tip: suck in the cheeks when applying darker make-up to the cheekbones . . . and apply only to the places that protrude. Bear in mind that white highlights bring out whatever you want to be seen. Darker make-up masks or shadows. Thus, on a large nose, using white make-up along the bridge of the nose and a base or brown shadow on the sides of the nose would minimize the appearance of the size of the nose itself. A touch of dark make-up on the nostrils will make them seem smaller, too.

Ditto the cheekbones. Darker shadow underneath the cheekbones, a white highlighter on the top of the cheekbones gives the appearance of higher cheekbones.

Minimizing the jaw with darker shadow is a trick that many proficient "T"s use. Blending in dark shadow on the boneline of each jaw makes the jaw "disappear" into the face or into the neck. This is easy to describe but takes a while to be able to do with discernable results.

Normally the eyes are the hardest part of the overall make-up opportunity—yet are the key to a well made-up face. What sort of eye shadow and mascara to use will be your own choice . . . and how to apply them as well as eyeliner will come with practice. This book is not designed to give you step-by-step procedure. The face of each person reading this is differ-ent so your own practice, along with some professional (or even nonprofessional) advice from others will be in order.

But bear in mind the use of dark and light shadows around the eyes, as described above, will go a long way toward highlighting the parts of the eyes you wish to be seen—and not seen. And as the eyes go, generally, so goes the facial appearance. If there's any sacrifice in time that you must make, always err in favor of the eyes. In this case, the eyes definitely have it.

Learning how to use mascara, getting it on and getting it off, is also an art. Putting mascara on the upper eyelids is usually not a difficult task. The lower eyelids take some practice . . . especially in how to use the end of the mascara brush to brush horizontally across the lower eyelashes. Their (lower eyelashes') short length makes it difficult to use the vertical stroke as you would the upper eyelashes.

Generally, the darker the lashes the more provocative the eyes look. A cardinal rule most "T"s follow is to use as much mascara as possible, right up to the point where it almost cakes.

A Quick Review

To achieve a natural glow, apply make-up over a light base of moisturizer, in the following order: 1) foundation, 2) blusher, 3) loose powder, 4) eye make-up, 5) lipstick. Here are a few step-by-step suggestions for your review. Because there have been so many books written on the subject, there's no need to go into great detail. Make-up will come easier to you after you experiment . . . which you'll do time and again.

Step one: <u>foundation</u>. Foundation will give you a smooth, one-color skin tone. But foundation also serves another purpose in that it can help moisturize and even protect the skin from the sun's rays.

The color foundation you use is important—and you might need some professional help in choosing the exact color to match your skin tone. If it's too dark, foundation looks mask-like. If it's too light it becomes chalky and you look unnatural.

As you tan during the summertime, change to a slightly darker foundation to match your skin tone.

Step 2: <u>blusher</u>. Blush is a perfect make-up to help accent your face shape or create contours. It also brings a gentle glow to the face.

There are various kinds of blushes, including cream blush for dry skin (which will also give you a touch of shine), and powder blush for normal-to-oily skin.

Blush should always complement your skin tone. A color consultant or make-up consultant can suggest the right color blush for you.

Step 3: <u>powder</u>. Loose powder is used to "set" the make-up . . . to keep it in place.

Powder will also keep your make-up looking fresh and natural throughout the day and evening.

Powder is best applied with a brush . . . some people "dot" powder over their make-up and blush, others brush it on in a downward motion.

Whichever system you use, make sure that you choose the same powder color as your foundation . . . or a colorless translucent type powder.

Step 4: <u>the eyes</u>. Take a look at your eyebrows. Are they too thick, do they look too masculine?

Today's fashion dictates a very natural look—not plucked thin eyebrows. Pencil thin lines are no longer in fashion . . . . . .but large thick eyebrows can ruin the look of any made-up face.

You can use eyebrow pencil to fill in the brows (should you be so lucky as to have thin brows) extending the line to a point that corresponds with the outer edge of the eye. A cardinal rule of using eyebrow pencil is to never use a black pencil unless your brows are naturally jet black. The pencil lines in the eyebrows should never show. In fact, for most "T"s, simply shaping the natural eyebrow is enough.

Eye shadow should be used very subtly. Natural shades are more fashionable and always look best for daytime.

Use eye shadow that flatters your eye color and skin tone. It is not particularly important to match the color of them with the color of your outfit.

Liquid eyeliner is very difficult to apply. But eyeliner pencil is easier, especially when you remember that the eyeliner should not appear as a specific line—but that it should only give the appearance of the darker color, thereby enlarging the eye.

Mascara is a must for everyone.

Step 6: <u>lipstick</u>. Lipstick is vital because it balances the effect of foundation, blusher, and eye make-up. Natural tones, soft pinks, peach, and clear light reds look good for most women during the day. In the evening, deepen the color.

Lip pencils should blend completely with the lipstick color you are wearing. Using a lip pencil will keep your lipstick from "bleeding" and to help enlarge or reduce the shape of your lips.

Lip gloss, applied evenly with a brush, is flattering to everyone. Use gloss alone for a natural look over lipstick for a special evening shine.

Bear in mind that night lighting fades out colors. At night you will need to touch up your basic make-up for evening wear, adding black or dark blue eye liner, a touch of deeper color to the crease of the eyelid, and a touch of paler color as a highlight under the eyebrow. You'll want to use more blush or a brighter color on cheeks for evenings, remembering that night lighting fades out colors. You'll also want to use a deeper or brighter lipstick at night, and possibly add gloss on top of it for real glamour.

Getting mascara off is usually the most difficult task in general make-up removal (and make-up should _always_ be removed completely before going to bed at night). Mascara remover, either in pads or in liquid form, is available in any drug store. Mascara remover makes the whole make-up removal process around the eyes much easier.

A rhythm of care

Doing make-up indeed wearing women's clothing—can soon evolve into a rhythm.

You will eventually design your own rhythm, but for most women the pattern goes something like this:

1) The night before, lay out things that you will wear the next day. That means everything—jewelry, belts, scarves, underwear. This will make dressing a pleasant experience, and your clothing message clear and deliberate right from the beginning.

You won't have to go through a pressing operation the next day, and you'll sleep better knowing that you won't have to make a lot of decisions immediately upon waking.

2) Do your hair and make-up before you dress so you won't get the clothes mussed and have to start all over again.

3) Protect your hair and make-up with a scarf when you pull clothing over your head.

4) Check yourself at least once before you put on your coat, and once afterwards.

You'll soon find that the whole routine shouldn't take more than thirty or forty minutes. But if you find that you are always rushing to get ready on time, start your day fifteen minutes earlier . . . start your make-up and clothing procedure earlier . . . and you'll feel much more on top of the situation.

Actresses and models, whose beauty is their profession, may spend an hour and a half getting dressed in the morning— but then they forget about it. You never see a confident woman primping, or touching her face or hair; most even try hard never to be caught looking in a mirror. The carefree and unself-conscious look is a large component of graceful beauty.

Additional thoughts

Many "T"s wear glasses.

Eye glasses tend to change the overall appearance—yet can be very feminine. Experimentation is the answer. It's been my experience that wearing glasses gives one the feeling of hiding. One's appearance may change so much (particularly if you don't wear glasses on a regular day-to-day situation as a male) that wearing them can be psychologically rewarding.

The current trend in eyeglasses is for the glasses to become more transparent—then the eyeglasses don't overcome your natural features.

Eyewear should act as an accessory to subtly match each outfit and occasion if possible.

Which frames are right for you? Again, it depends on your mood. For a splash of color, look for frames with tones on the upper-outer edge that accentuate your gaze and add a lift to your face.

A soft, rectangular style generally looks good on all face shapes, but if you have sharp, square features, look for frames with rounder corners (vice-versa for full faces.) The ideal eye wear features frames that play up (not hide) your face.

Experience in buying glasses can be traumatic— particularly the first few times you buy them. Prior to my being able to go into a store and buy glasses directly as a woman, I used a number of methods of buying glasses. For example, I would tell the optometrist I was doing a play and I needed the glasses for the woman's part I was taking in the play. Or I would tell him that I was doing an after-dinner speech, playing the part of a "madam chairman" and needed feminine glasses.

Buying glasses as a woman was simple. While I received my prescription from the ophthalmologist as a man, I simply added "Mrs." to the name. The eye glass franchisee was happy to accept the prescription . . . and having the prescription in the woman's name simply added to the attribution already made by the salesperson in the eye glass store that I was, indeed, the woman I presented.

But again, remember, whatever ex-cuse or reason you use, optometrists-employees simply want to sell eyeglasses. If you want to buy glasses and are frightened to do so, remember the major problem is theirs, not yours. Any reason you use to buy glasses is good enough for them—they want to make the sale. Or have we said that before somewhere???

Watch the ladies

Something else I've mentioned before in this book—and I will mention again—is that I strongly urge you to buy Vogue magazine or other fashion magazines, from time to time. Look at the pictures of the ladies—pay particular attention to their make-up. You'll find that most of them are not overdone . . . even though they may be rather heavily made up.

Pay attention to the make-up, down to the most tiny detail. Use these models as models for yourself. For example, try to do your lips the same way models do. Note that lip make-up will vary from model to model, picture to picture. Experiment—experiment—experiment . . . try a number of different ways of applying lipstick until you find one that feels comfortable. The same advice would apply to mascara, eye shadow, eye liner, foundation, blush, or any other make-up you might wish to apply and yet are not sure how it should look.

Also watch women on the street or in any kind of social situation. Notice how their make-up changes according to the time of day—more make-up in the evening, less during the day. Notice what they wear at work—notice how and when they apply their make-up. Watch how women reapply their make-up after a meal.

Note that most women apply their lipstick and/or power at the table after a meal . . . rather than apply their make-up when they go into the ladies room. These methods vary, of course, but by being observant you'll soon note what the other women are doing, and you'll do likewise.

Incidentally, applying your make-up before you go into the ladies room is another good idea . . . it keeps you from prolonging your visit into what could be a dangerous situation. One more in a line of practical tips from someone who has been there.

Finally, an additional way to keep people from analyzing your make-up too carefully . . . is to smile. I'll continue to mention it, but women do smile at other women . . . and especially at children. Women generally do not smile, on the street, at men. Those kinds of smiles can be taken for something they actually aren't. But a woman smiling at another woman gets a smile in return—not a close look at make-up, dress, or other aspects of the person coming toward them or sitting across from them. And when people are smiling at who you are, they will not be wondering what you are.

Chapter 5

Body Language

Women come in all shapes and sizes.

There are women with wide hips, women with narrow hips, women with big busts and women less well-endowed. Some women have large hands, some have dainty, delicate hands. Some women have full, rounded faces, others have thin, angular faces.

Contrary to the myth of the Perfect 10, most women live with a combination of physical imperfections.

"Ts" typically visualize the ideal woman and then attempt to fashion themselves in her image. No harm in trying.

The experienced "T" understands her limitations and knows that she will simply have to do the best she can with what she's got. The end result will fall short of perfect, according to Tinsel Town standards, but will approach, if not surpass, the appearance of the vast majority of women walking the streets.

"T"s create and project an image—the perception of the viewer becomes reality.

What the viewer sees is what the viewer gets. By paying particular attention to the parts of the body that can be feminized, the clever and resourceful "T" creates the illusion of a very feminine woman.

Women suffer far more than men do from a sense of inadequacy about their bodies, the conditioned response to centuries of service in the role of sex object and ornament. Almost every woman is insecure about at least one aspect of her body. That insecurity can transform self-image and in turn, reality.

When a "T" understands and accepts the fact that many women are insecure about their bodies, she will begin to develop a sense of security about the parts of her body that are not as "perfect" as she might like. After all, if women were more comfortable with their bodies they might flatter and enhance rather than hide and disguise them.

For most of their lives, women labor to live up to society's image of the Perfect 10.

The 36"-24"-36" model seems to be the standard expectation, abetted by constant comparisons with models in Vogue or centerfolds in Playboy magazine.

As fashion trends change different body types come in and out of style, from Twiggy to Roseanne. There is no way to win the "perfect body" game.

Ironically, here's where "Ts" have an advantage. Pads and other aids can help "Ts" to conform with the latest fashion trends, particularly because "Ts" can enhance body parts that women, according to the dictates of fashion, can't.

Self-acceptance comes hard for women, considering their struggle to transcend and grow beyond the very narrow and limiting expectations imposed on their image, worth and value by male-dominated cultures. As a "woman," a "T" should give herself credit for coming as far as she has with her own self-acceptance.

As a "T", you probably harbor a deeply imprinted sense of inadequacy about your image of yourself as a woman. You can soften that insecurity by learning how to express the complete, undiminished, exciting you, and by learning how to diminish the power of other people's expectations.

So, let's take a look at the various parts of the body to learn how you, as a "T", can enhance those parts to create the whole and total woman.

Hands

It is easy to say that hands are hands, that you really can't do much about them.

Actually, there are steps that you can take to make your hands more presentable. (How to carry the hands, how to hold them and what to do with them while walking, sitting, and talking will be discussed in Chapter 7).

Women don't have an abundance of hair on their hands and arms. What hair there is is usually in the form of "peach fuzz" or nearly-invisible hair.

How often have we seen "Ts" who are dressed almost to perfection only to be exposed by the tell-tale black hair on the back of their hands or on their arms? Nothing is more revealing and nothing is easier to remedy.

Shave the hair on the back of the hands, shave it up as high as you have to.

If you are afraid that someone will notice that the hair on your hands has been shaved, shave it a bit at a time. As it disappears gradually it won't be noticed. This is another example of "planning ahead," a concept referred to in previous and in following chapters. "It ain't easy being a girl," but if you are shackled by the problem of attempting to hide the hair on your hands, you are fighting an impossible, uphill battle. Of course, you could go around with your palms up, but people would talk. It's hard enough as it is.

Sure, you can wear long-sleeved blouses, dresses or sweaters to cover hairy arms. Lots of part-time "Ts" do so but they definitely, but definitely, shave the back of their hands and the hair up to and above the wrist.

Maybe you're one of those lucky ones without much hair, or perhaps your hair is light enough that an application or two of bleach will do the trick. Experimentation is the answer.

As you grow into a more feminine sense of self, pay attention to other women. You will notice that they often push their sleeves up or wear short or three-quarter length sleeves. Exposing your wrists allows you to display your jewelry, creating the effect of smaller wrists and slimmer arms.

Again, bleaching hair helps, but for most "Ts", the eventual solution is shaving or otherwise removing the arm hairs. Luckily, arms don't have to be shaved as often as, say, the legs. The good news is that genetic women have hair on their arms. You're going to look so pretty that nobody's going to notice the little bit of fuzz on your arms once you've done what you can to minimize it.

Hand Cream

It may seem late in life to begin to think about smooth, soft skin. If you have not been using a hand cream during the day and particularly at night, then it's time you began. Every little bit helps.

Hand creams aren't magic. If you're an auto mechanic by day, chances are that all the skin cream in the world won't make your hands soft for evening outings.

Begin to use hand cream on a daily basis. Even if your "T" activities go no further, your skin will be a lot softer in the long run.

Nails

Most women don't wear colored nail polish. They seem to find it too difficult to put on, too difficult to maintain and simply don't want to go to the trouble.

More and more women wear clear polish, basically to protect their nails, give them a sheen and make them look more presentable.

Chances are that as a "T" you'll want to use polish. It tends to elongate the fingers, making your entire hand look smaller. (Okay, we admit it. By and large, "Ts" have larger hands than genetic women. I'd like to alter that fact but I can't. What I can do is offer some suggestions for making your hands look thinner and more feminine).

Ideally, you can grow your own nails long enough, shape them yourself and paint them to create the effect of a professional manicure.

But on a practical basis, living a day-to-day masculine existence with long nails is difficult.

I have found that I can let my nails grow, keep them relatively squared off until a few days before my "T" activity, then let them grow more pointed and finally, shape them into a more feminine style prior to doing my own manicure. No one has ever said anything to me about the shape or length of my nails.

Putting on fingernail polish is a science, one that demands artful practice. Sometimes you'll fall in love with one particular type of polish (changing shades for various occasions as you experiment), using it and again as you will other types of make-up. Some women believe in applying only one coat of polish but it's been my experience that two or three coats seem to do a better job. I always finish with a clear cover coat in order to protect the manicure.

The press-on nails that are now available are better than ever before. They stay on longer, have a more attractive shape, are available in many colors and come in sizes large enough for "Ts" to use.

Naturally, they'll pop off at just the wrong time no matter what precautions you take. Carry an extra set or two in your purse. There's nothing more embarrassing or nerve-wracking than having a nail pop off, losing it, and having no replacement.

There are, of course, the glue-on nails . . . nails that require strong adhesives such as Krazy Glue to keep them in place.

These nails will stay on longer than the press-on type, but they're much more difficult to remove. As with the acrylic tips mentioned below, you'll need to find a solvent such as acetone to remove the fingernails (and the glue). (A personal note: it's always nice to think about how you're going to get the nails off before you put them on. The first and only time I neglected to do so was during the excitement of one of my first acrylic tip applications by a manicurist. About two hours before I had to revert back to my masculine "drag," I realized that simple polish remover wasn't going to do the trick. I needed solvent, but by that time it was too late to get some. I had to cut and scrape the nails and I wound up sitting on my hands for the next two days. A word to the wise: plan ahead!)

Short of having your own nails, the ideal way to have your nails look and feel good (and I've found that the better your nails look and feel, the better presentation you make) is to have them done professionally by a manicurist.

It isn't cheap. A complete set of nails may well run you as much as $45 or $50—but it's worth it. They look absolutely beautiful and without a doubt can be one of the most attractive and flattering aspects of your appearance.

Where to find a manicurist? Just about anywhere! By asking your "T" friends you'll be able to find a manicurist who will be happy to do your nails, either with a regular manicure or with the acrylic tips. If it makes you feel better, you can always use the old excuse that you're going to a party and would like to have your nails done after you've dressed. Money talks, and you'll discover more than a few manicurists who'll be happy to do your nails and won't blink an eye even if they know you're not a genetic female.

As you become more accomplished at dressing and more confident about passing, your fears about getting a manicure will soften. You may feel reluctant to use your masculine voice on the phone. No problem—simply make an appointment for "your wife." Better yet, if you look and feel good, sashay right into any manicurist shop and make your own appointment. Sounds like simple advice, but many "Ts" hesitate to go to beauty shops or manicurists. Trust me—they'll be happy for your business.

Hair

Yes, it's nice to use your own hair, to let it grow, to curl it, to have it done professionally. Nice but . . .

Most genetic males simply don't have enough hair. Either that . . . or they don't have the freedom and flexibility to let it grow as long as they would like. The reality is that most "Ts" use wigs of one kind or another.

I am being kind in this chapter by not going into great depth on the subject of Male Pattern Baldness. If you are going to be bald you are going to be bald. Most "Ts" don't start female hormones until long after the Male Pattern Baldness syndrome has taken effect. Consequently, most "Ts" just don't have enough hair, period.

Hair transplants

Hair grows softer and more luxuriant when female hormones are taken, but most "Ts" will never get to that stage.

Because Male Pattern Baldness is going to overtake most "Ts", there is another answer—hair transplants.

At a cost of $15-25 per plug (each plug taken from the back of the head has 10-15 hairs in it), as many as 300-500 plugs can be removed from the back of the head and inserted into the front or balding part of the head.

The result can be a luxurious flow of hair, particularly effective if the "T" wishes to use her own hair at a later date.

From personal experience I can tell you that there is relatively little pain involved. If you decide to have hair transplants, have them done by an expert. Your best bet is a transplant clinic. As with any medical procedures mentioned in this book, get recommendations from other "Ts" who have actually used a particular surgeon.

If you have enough hair of your own, you represent the "T" ideal. Remember, many women have short hair. It's amazing how little hair you need, as long as its done professionally. Over the years we've watched "Ts" reach the point of making a visit to the beauty salon, having their own hair done and then venturing out for the first time without a wig. That's an exciting achievement in any "Ts" life. While some of us will never be able to do it, kudos to those who can.

Oh, yes,—there are plenty of hairdressers happy to do a "T"'s hair. Just ask—business is business is business. And remember, you can always ask the other "Ts" in your support group to help you to an obliging hairdresser.

Wigs

You don't have to spend a lot of money on wigs. I've owned fifteen or twenty in my lifetime, but now I'm down to three Eva Gabor wigs, all the same style, each with a price tag of less than $75 (that's after paying literally hundreds of dollars for human hair wigs made specifically for me).

Acrylic wigs are truly fantastic! Synthetic hair not only looks good but is easy to care for. It can be washed in minutes, hung or placed on a wig rack immediately and as soon as it's completely dry, it can be combed out by even the novice T.

These synthetic wigs are available in any color and in any style. You can purchase them to match your own hair, which gives you the advantage of combing your own hair right into the wig, removing that tell-tale line between face and hair.

If there's any one tip-off that reveals a wig it's the absence of a hairline. Understanding this simple fact when you purchase your wig gives you an advantage that most first-time wig buyers don't have.

You can, of course, buy wigs through catalogs, through ads that appear in publications like Tapestry and other "T" publications. Practically every major department store has a wig boutique. Again, without experience, you'll probably be too frightened to make a wig purchase yourself. But once you muster your courage, understanding again that people are there to make sales and not to criticize, you'll be able to go in and try on various wigs. The salesperson is a professional. He or she will make sure that you get something that fits your face or that matches your own hair, something that looks good on you.

The face

The bane of existence for many "T"'s is the beard.

Much has been written on the removal of the beard. In fact, there are as many theories about how to remove five o'clock shadow as there are individuals who have it. And that includes most genetic males.

Obviously you'll want to shave as closely as possible.

Shaving close is an art, and practice makes perfect. A sharp razor and a soft beard make for the closest shave and the smoothest skin. Don't fuss with electric razors—they don't get close enough.

Advanced "Ts" who still need to shave have learned to shave twice—once with the grain of the hair (the way it grows) and then again against the grain. The second shave seems to get much deeper than the first, which keeps the beard from growing out as rapidly as it would after only one shave.

The normal male beard usually needs to be shaved twice a day if a "T" intends to spend the entire day dressed. I never realized this (believing that my foundation make-up would cover my five o'clock shadow—I didn't have a particularly heavy beard) until one day I asked a close friend to look closely for any signs of a shadow on my face. This was before the days of my electrolysis, but I was confident that my friend would see no shadow. Much to

my dismay, he saw a five o'clock shadow. (It was evening, and I hadn't shaved since the morning.) Even with a relatively light-colored beard, even having shaved very closely both with and against the grain, I still had a shadow towards the end of the day. This shadow appeared to the observant viewer despite the fact that I wore a special cover-up make-up over the worst parts of my beard and then covered that with a foundation, blusher, powder, the works.

The moral of my story is obvious—it is very very difficult, no matter how much you work on it, to shave only once a day and have the shave last throughout an entire day and evening. There is no solution to this problem other than electrology.

Electrolysis

Electrolysis is a long and painful process. It's been my experience that only those "Ts" who are quite serious ever begin (and finish) the electrology process.

One good electrology session has cured many a "T" of the idea. The cost of electrolysis—in dollars and in physical pain--has sent many a "T" desperate to be rid of unwanted facial hair back to the razor and shaving twice a day.

There's nothing very exciting about the electrology process . . . including the time that it takes. While some luckier individuals (and I thank my stars that I was one of those) can remove the entire beard in a hundred hours or less of electrology, I've talked to many, many "Ts" who have had as much as four or five hundred hours of work done . . . and are still not finished with the process. That's called dedication—painful, expensive dedication.

Consider the fact that electrology can cost from $40 to $80 an hour. You can begin to see that in addition to the hassle and pain, the expense is nothing to sneeze at.

Many "Ts" undergoing electrology experience a swelling reaction to the process. Unless a lot of time and effort is taken to minimize the swelling by using cold compresses or icepacks on the area for an hour or two after the electrology process, there seems to be no avoiding a two or three day fat lip—or cheek.

Another time-consuming factor to consider when evaluating electrology as an option is beard growth. In order to be able to reach the hair follicles easily, the electrologist asks that the client not shave for a day or two prior to the process. Again, this requirement causes a lot of schedule juggling for those who must be clean-shaven in their work as a male.

How about regrowth? Yes, the hair does tend to come back, primarily hairs that have not been disabled in the electrology process. The regrowth problem is discouraging. Just when you think you've gotten everything cleared up, along comes a number of black hairs. It's almost a process of two steps forward, one step back.

Electrologists will remove the black hairs first. The beard has a number of black hairs along with white hairs, depending on the age of the client. White hair doesn't show as much under make-up, which is why it's the last to go. As the black hairs are removed, the "T" very quickly sees the difference in the five o'clock shadow. A light shaving of the white hairs will last a day or two until the time when they're removed.

The question that "Ts" undergoing electrology must answer is how far to take the electrology. After the face, chin and neck are completed, does the "T" go ahead and have the electrologist work on removing the chest hairs? How about the arms? The legs? The back?

I have talked to a number of "Ts" who draw the line at the neck, satisfied to stop at completing a course of facial electrology. Most "Ts" find that they can get by shaving or waxing their legs, arms and chest (although waxing the chest is so painful I wouldn't recommend it to anyone but the most avowed masochist).

Where do you find an electrologist?

First bear in mind that electrologists are used to working on "Ts". Practically any electrologist you approach will be happy to have you as a client.

Also remember that there are good, bad, and indifferent electrologists. Here's where your support group comes in—here's where you need to discuss the various capabilities of electrologists in your geographical area. Remember, cost isn't necessarily the most important criterion . . . many electrologists who charge less take many more hours, have a more painful process, and simply aren't as efficient as others. Again: compare—compare—compare.

You can trust your professional electrologist (after making sure he or she is a member of their state and/or national electrologist association). Bear in mind that their business calls for privacy—they won't talk about you and your needs. They can't, because if they did they'd soon be out of business.

When looking for an electrologist, find out the type of electrology they do. There are various methods, each with varying degrees of danger for burning the skin, each with varying thresholds of pain, each with regrowth differentiation. Ask your fellow "T"'s about the type of system used, ask about success ratios. There is nothing like experience in dealing with an electrologist.

A final note about electrology. Although it doesn't sound like a very happy story, the result, if you have a lot of patience, pain tolerance, and money, can be well worth it. Throughout the electrology process the client feels that she's getting something accomplished—getting closer to the day when she can throw the razor out the window, closer to the day when she won't need pounds of pancake to cover her beard. Bear in mind, as we said in the make-up section earlier, that most women on the street use very little, if any, make-up. Beginning "Ts" use a lot of make-up but as they get better, they use less and less. A "T" who has had a complete electrology job often finds herself using no foundation at all—just some lipstick, eye make-up, and out she goes.

Electrology does give you freedom. In the long run, the electrology process and the facials that you'll have afterwards are probably good for the skin. So bear with it, patience is a virtue.

One final point on the subject. If you are planning on electrology and begin the female hormone treatment, it is best to get as much of the electrology done as possible prior to the beginning of the hormonal treatment. The theory is that female hormones make the skin more tender and that having taken hormones, "Ts" are much less able to tolerate the pain involved. This is an especially important and sensitive point for those who plan to have electrology in their breast area.

Eyebrows

Eyebrows are usually a dead giveaway on novice "Ts"—they are simply too thick.

Eyebrows must be trimmed, but they don't have to be pencil thin to be tasteful and attractive.

Get a Vogue magazine and look at the models. They don't have thin arched eyebrows. They usually have eyebrows that mold to the face . . . more good news for "Ts".

Electrologists, even beauticians, are used to thinning eyebrows and cutting them to shape. Of course you can pluck your own eyebrows—as well as trim them. Plucking is painful but it works. Again, artful plucking is a matter of practice. Other women get good at it—so will you. Remember that in most cases, the eyebrow should extend beyond the eyes themselves. Check with a make-up artist or professional beautician for advice on the width and length of your eyebrows.

The hands

The narrower the wrist, the smaller the appearance of the hand. One way to achieve this effect is to wear bracelets, remembering that nothing looks worse on a big hand or a big wrist than a bracelet that is too tight. Try to get bracelets that are big enough and loose enough to give the wrist a slimmer look.

Wearing too much jewelry, particularly finger rings, tends to draw attention to the hands. (A cardinal rule for wearing jewelry is to put on all the jewelry you wish, then to remove at least one piece.)

If you are going to wear rings, perhaps you should try a wedding ring. A wedding ring or wedding band adds to the illusion of womanhood, creating the impression of marriage. Every little aspect of the overall presentation is helpful—often, a wedding band will cause the casual observer to lose interest. So if limited interest and anonymity is what you want, see if you can find an engagement ring and a wedding band.

Additional rings will only call attention to the hands. If your heart is set on more, limit it to one ring on the opposite hand.

Legs and Arms

Women generally have smooth legs.

They don't come that way naturally, they get that way with shaving or waxing, sometimes by using depilatories, a chemical process which dissolves the root of the hair and which lasts about as long as tweezing or waxing.

When a "T" shaves her legs for the first time she's in for an initial shock. Hair, after all, is a part of our bodies and we tend to get used to it.

For most males, shaved legs are difficult to hide in a male environment . . . or even in a family environment where "T" activities are not openly acknowledged. There are many limitations on social activities when legs and arms are clear of hair.

Remember, though, that hair on the arms and legs does return, usually in three or four days at best, perhaps after one or two days at worst. Many women have to shave their legs on a daily basis,

particularly if their legs show and they're concerned about keeping them looking smooth and clear of hair.

Shaving the legs gets easier and easier with practice. It takes only a minute or two to shave the legs . . . and the well-organized "T" has leg shaving down to a science. Most "Ts" use one razor to shave their legs and a different razor to shave their face. You'll want a sharper blade for your face. Shaving the legs tends to dull the blades more quickly.

A much longer term answer is waxing. A professional wax job can last as long as five or six weeks.

Waxing certainly costs more than shaving but the effect lasts longer, not to mention other beneficial attributes. Waxing the arms or legs removes dead skin as well as unwanted hair. Ostensibly, the skin ends up in better shape after waxing than after shaving.

There is little, if any, pain in waxing, with the exception of the chest area.

Some electrologists offer waxing in addition to their electrolysis services. They usually offer facial and skin care tips too. You can typically trust electrologists to be good waxers. Waxing is also done in many beauty salons.

Some electrologists believe that coil hair-removing machines as well as waxing will damage hair follicles, cause ingrown hairs, and make future electrolysis more difficult.

Many "Ts" do their own waxing, after some initial supervision. Some "Ts" even wax their beards, a relatively painful process but one that keeps the face cleaner than shaving for a few days or possibly a week.

There's a running debate on the issue

of waxed hair growing back quicker and thicker than the original hair. Some electrologists and skin care professionals argue that hair that is waxed grows back more sparsely after waxing, that waxing removes beginning hairs that would have served to thicken the hair. It has been my personal experience that waxing does last longer and that the hair does grow back thinner. My arms and legs are waxed every six to eight weeks, but I still shave them if I notice hairs showing through my hosiery or on my bare arms.

Have you seen the new hair removing devices which use a moving coil spring to automatically pull out the hair? They work on the arms or on the legs . . . doesn't hurt very much and accomplishes the same result as waxing.

Those who have used these devices tell me that the effects last longer than shaving, a little less longer than waxing. . at a cost considerably less expensive than waxing. Of course the benefit through waxing of removing dead skin doesn't happen with use of the machine. But for day-in and day-out use, you might find that they are the perfect tool for keeping your hair off at a price you can afford.

The chest
Here's a part of the body that's very difficult for most "Ts" to hide.

Most men have hair on their chest. By wearing open shirts and living in the male-oriented world they have revealed (and sometimes reveled in) the hair on their chests. To shave the hair and to then return to a male-oriented world without it is awkward, to say the least.

It is even more awkward to be seen by others when the shaved hair has grown back partially. There doesn't seem to be much of a long-term answer other than electrolysis and/or waxing, neither a thrilling proposition.

Chest hair seems to come back quicker than leg or arm hair, and it is difficult to maintain a clear chest. If a "T" plans to wear a low-cut dress and to show cleavage, she will find it necessary to shave her chest hair practically every day. It isn't easy being a girl . . .

Cleavage is not easy to develop, either.

There are many techniques to show cleavage, including wrapping the breasts very tightly with an ace bandage, forcing the body fat into the center of the chest and then wearing a bra and prostheses in such a way that they don't show but the cleavage does.

In her book Art and Illusion Joanne Roberts shows a technique using sport tape (used to wrap the wrists and ankles of athletes) and Mole skin (used to cushion bunions and other foot problems). Joanne's system calls for the tape to be placed under the nipples, then the skin of the breast to be pulled together by the Mole skin. Pulling the flesh of the chest together creates a cleft.

In the final analysis, cleavage is going to be based on the amount of body fat you have. If you don't have enough body fat in the breast area you're not going to have cleavage no matter what action you take.

Using make-up to contour and highlight the cleavage will help the illusion. Add shadow in the cleft and highlight the top curve of the breast for maximum effect.

Most "Ts" don't have much success in creating cleavage. But if it works it may be worth the effort. The lower cut dresses or blouses that you can wear will pull the viewer's eye downwards, thereby minimizing (in the eyes of the beholder) the size of the shoulders and upper torso.

If you can't develop cleavage, don't lose any sleep over it. Most women seldom show it anyway.

A personal note—never, <u>NEVER</u>, use adhesive tape directly on your skin. I once tried it under each nipple, then joined the two with additional adhesive tape across the front of the chest. I had cleavage, all right, and also three red marks that lasted over six months when my skin came off with the adhesive tape. I should have known better.

The rear

Seems like women these days have bigger and bigger hips . . . or are those just the ones walking in front of us?

Then again, some women have hardly any hips at all.

A cardinal rule when thinking about your rear end is: don't worry about it too much. You probably have slimmer hips than you might like. Yet unless you build yourself up too big in the bust area, your hips as they are will be similar to those of most other women.

You can, of course, wear pads under your panty girdles. Foam rubber pads are readily available in shops that cater to "Ts" and in specialty stores such as Frederick's of Hollywood. Frederick's also carries panty girdles with built-in hip pads, but they seldom accomplish the look that "Ts" aspire to achieve (more hips in the rear, a more rounded contour shape).

As of this writing, nobody I know has come up with a panty girdle with built-in hip pads and thigh pads that give the totally rounded shape so many "Ts" prefer.

One of the problems with foam rubber pads is the difficulty aligning them and then keeping them in place. In fact, realigning hip pads after bathroom use is often very difficult and sometimes virtually impossible, particularly if some other lady is waiting to get into the stall. On occasion I've become so frustrated and flustered by this problem (yes, I'm one of those who wears hip pads) that I have simply removed the pads, put them in my very large purse, and spent the rest of the day without them, replacing them when I have some privacy and time.

Once you begin to wear hip pads you'll need to stay with it if you have bought dresses and skirts to fit the size of those hips. At a minimum you'll have to wear the pads when you wear those articles of clothing.

Again, as we've said so many times before and will continue to repeat, as "Ts" get more comfortable they wear less and less padding. I suspect that there are very few post-operative "Ts" who wear any padding at all. On a practical basis it makes little difference. On a psychological basis, when you don't feel you need to wear padding you've really arrived.

Breasts

Breasts, like women, come in all different sizes and shapes.

In talking about breasts I'm always reminded of an old joke: What do a breast and a martini have in common? One's not enough and three are too many.

Some "Ts" often look as if they are

carrying three breasts, confusing breast size with femininity.

The major point (no pun intended) to remember about breast size is "not too big, not too high."

Women's breasts should strike at about the middle of the upper arm when the arm is held along the side of the body.

The older a woman, the lower her breasts normally hang. Despite this, some older "Ts" persist in maintaining breasts at an 18-year-old level. It's a dead give-away that the breasts aren't real.

Breasts that are too large for the torso bring the viewer's attention to the upper body, the last place to which most "Ts" want to draw attention. Very accomplished "Ts" wear almost no padding or prostheses at all; they're content to live with an A cup.

Women's breasts are not pointed, they are round. Women wear bras to give their breasts support, and the bras round off the nipple so that it doesn't show, even through very light blouses. Overly pointed breasts are another giveaway.

The price of artificial breast prostheses can run from as little as $50 a pair on up to thousands of dollars, depending on quality and size. Generally, the more you pay the better. Silicone-filled mastectomy forms are usually the best bet.

The most comfortable weight for prostheses is the weight closest to that of real breasts. If you are going to be involved in the "T" odyssey to any extent, you should be willing to spend what it takes to get comfortable, authentic looking and feeling breasts.

Buying breasts, not only for size but for weight, feel, and wear is a task that benefits from advice.

Prostheses can be bought from many foundation garment shops, or you can look in the yellow pages of the phone book. People who sell prostheses are used to selling to "Ts"; just tell them why you need them and they'll be happy to do business.

Again, your support group can point you to the best place to buy prostheses as well as other equipment that will be helpful as you make the transition from man to woman.

When I first began dressing, because I am so tall and relatively large-framed, I wore a D cup. My first purchase of a good set of prostheses moved me down to a C cup. But even with a C cup, I found that buying dresses and blouses to fit my large frame, particularly when the C cup is added on to the width of my body, became a very difficult process. I simply couldn't find a selection of clothes that fit. The breasts got in my way as I went about my daily business, and, darn it, they were heavy. Switching to the more expensive, silicon form-filled mastectomy forms, I moved down to a B cup (A is next). The result? I feel much better about how I look. Of course I don't notice my breasts as much, but neither does the observer. That's good for both of us.

The tummy

You knew I was going to say it . . . there are heavy women and there are heavy men.

Typically, as people approach mid-life their weight moves toward their middle.

Yes, I know you have always wanted to wear a girdle; there's something about a girdle or a corset that appeals to every beginning "T".

But as any woman and most accomplished "Ts" will tell you, nothing is more uncomfortable to wear over a long period of time than a girdle, corset, waist cincher or any kind of a garment that restricts your movement. ("My girdle is KILLING me," she whispered.)

I know that and you know that, but chances are you're still going to want to wear a girdle. It adds to the illusion, it gives you the feeling of being slim and svelte, it makes you feel and look younger. A girdle can also be a good reminder that a slimmer body would not only look nicer but feel better. That girdle just might get you started on the diet you've been thinking about.

Panty girdles that come halfway up the tummy can add to your discomfort and detract from your appearance. They tend to roll over, and the bulk of the girdle adds girth to your tummy.

There are so many problems in getting corsets to fit that I won't elaborate other than to remind you again that if you're going to be out dressed for any length of time (especially if you're uncomfortable in corsets or girdles), you need to make some basic choices. Bear in mind that there are many heavy women. A tummy just might add to your authenticity.

The Adam's apple

The Adam's apple or the trachea protrudes more on most men than it does on women.

On the other hand, many "Ts" are lucky and have little if any protruding Adam's apple.

For the vast majority of "Ts", unless they plan to go all the way through trans-sexual reassignment surgery, nothing can or should be done about a protruding Adam's apple.

There are ways to minimize the problem, including high-necked dresses, blouses, turtleneck sweaters or other clothing that hides the Adam's apple.

Careful application of make-up can also minimize an Adam's apple. Use a darker make-up to hide the protrusion and apply lighter make-up around it to create a more one-dimensional look.

The operation to remove the Adam's apple is called the tracheal scrape.

The medical term for the operation is "laryngeal-chondroplasty."

The surgery is performed with the smallest possible incision to avoid scarring. Care must be taken not to touch the voice box, which is typically level with the base of the Adam's apple. This lump is cartilage, which is removed. The procedure is done under a local anesthetic and takes about an hour. Recovery time is an estimated seven to ten days. The cost runs from $1,000-2,000.

The operation must be done by a qualified surgeon; it's very often done during a face lift or other cosmetic surgery. A tracheal scrape leaves a very small scar. Usually the outside skin is cut on the fold of the neck. The scar disappears over a period of a few weeks. Most tracheal scrapes that I've seen on "Ts" have been very successful.

Facelifts

Speaking of surgery, have you considered a facelift lately?

For "T"s approaching forty-something and beyond, a facelift is not only in order, it will make a dramatic difference in overall appearance.

If you are planning a facelift, letting a qualified plastic surgeon know that you are a "T" (even if you don't plan to go all the way on the spectrum) is recommended. When the surgeon is aware of your goal, he or she can design a more feminine face for you.

There are a multitude of benefits from facelifts, not the least of which are psychological. When you look better, you feel better.

There are other cosmetic advantages to plastic surgery. When loose skin is cut away electrolysis is easier. Facelifts generally call for the removal of a large amount of facial skin. Sounds horrible, but it works, as thousands upon thousands of people discover to their delight each year.

You might think about partial facelifts on the eyes or cheeks. Bags under the eyes and drooping eyelids have been transformed by plastic surgeons to the benefit of many "Ts" who look both younger—and more feminine.

As Dr. Maxwell Maltz proved in his book Psycho-cybernetics, we are what we look like. As we feel better we become a better woman, and a better "T".

Sideburns

Sideburns always seem to be a problem with "Ts", particularly "Ts" who move in and out of the male world.

Since women don't have sideburns, "Ts" must either shave them off or wear wigs that cover them. Getting a wig to cover sideburns is practically impossible.

Women's hair seems to grow to the top of the ear, and rarely lower. A common trick that many "Ts" use on sideburns consists of shaving them gradually,

a little more each day or week, a process that makes for a subtle change in the eyes of the casual observer. Once the sideburns are gone, the hair at the top of the sideburn is grown long and combed back over the ears, creating the perfect effect for hair that will comb right into a wig to make it look more authentic.

Genital area

"Ts" are always aware of their genitals and ever fearful that they will show.

Unless you're unusually well-endowed, a panty girdle is normally enough to hide the genital area.

Remember that a woman's genital area protrudes, too; it doesn't disappear entirely between her legs.

Genital pads are available but they usually make the situation worse. Simply look at yourself, or ask someone else if they think you protrude too much.

It is best to ignore this problem, basically because it isn't a problem, at least not one that generally shows.

Feet

People won't tend to look at your feet, unless your shoes are unusual or clash with your outfit. Only during the summertime, when you might wear open-toed shoes, will your toes show.

Painting the toenails is more trouble than it's worth, particularly for "Ts" who have to go back into the masculine world.

Painted toenails also make your feet look longer. On the other hand, if you want longer feet, have at it.

Hosiery and shoes will cover unsightly hair on the feet, but the same rule applies for feet that does for legs—waxing, shaving, and coil type hair removal machines or a depilatory can remove unwanted hair. Most "Ts" pay little attention to what their feet look like, except for the proper shoes, of course.

Conclusion

One of the great advantages of being a "T" is the opportunity to treat your body as it should have been treated—and probably wasn't—for many years.

You will find that you appreciate your body more because you are paying more attention than ever before.

In the process of working on your body you tend to get healthier, just one more benefit on this path.

Chapter 6

The Voice

Three things you can be judged by—your voice, your face, and your disposition.
—Ignas Bernstein

Gentle, and low, an excellent thing in a woman.
—Shakespeare, King Lear,

Of all the transformations implicit and explicit, voice control is perhaps the easiest physically and the most difficult psychologically, to achieve.

Why is it so difficult for "T"s to control their voices-to "change" them so that they sound more feminine?

Perhaps we harbor a natural reluctance to "pretend" to be something we're not by talking in a way that diverges from the longstanding tones and patterns of speech we're used to. Or perhaps the difficulty is a more practical one—most men have a larger larynx area or voice box grid. Perhaps it's a combination of mental and physical factors. If the eyes are the window of the soul, the voice gives the soul its expression. Femininizing the voice or changing it in any way, for that matter, is psychologically difficult for anyone.

"Giving expression to the soul" is another way of saying that the feminine expression of voice is ultimately the expression of your identity.

For whatever reason, "T"s often feel that using a softer or more feminine voice exposes the transformation. Or they may feel that the inner voice is truly feminine. Many "T"s, who will go to great lengths to change their appearance, still can't overcome the psychological impediments that block voice change. We often recognize that there are many women with deeper voices than ours. We listen to actresses such as Marlene Dietrich, Carol Channing, Talullah Bankhead and others. Or, while listening to women talk, we hear all sorts of pitches, resonance, low voices, raspy sounds, breathy, harsh, shrill, and commanding tones, all attributes that we can use to make our masculine voices sound feminine.

With a little knowledge, some changes in vocabulary and a great deal of practice, the masculine voice can be feminized.

The words of Anne Bolin in her book In Search of Eve are appropriate:

Voice and speech patterns do not progress as rapidly as appearance in the passing arena, and much initial public passing is traumatic for "T"s because of this. Perfection in speech takes some time and practice for most. Apart from recognizing that pitch and tone in most cases need to be raised, "T"s are aware of para-linguistic and sociolinguistic gender disparities in speech. They know that females generally raise pitch at the end of a sentence and use tag questions, such as "isn't it?" They are also sensitive to female lexical usage. They consciously use weaker expletives, choosing to be generally more polite than males, and they opt for women's adjectives such as lovely, cute, darling and the like, which, if used by males, would impugn their integrity. These "T"s are not participating in a feminist speech revolution; they simply want to pass. They practice female voice and speech patterns until they become habitual and are no longer a conscious effort.

Physiological differences

Yes, there are physiological differences, real anatomical differences in the speech mechanisms of the sexes.

Probably the definitive guide on the subject is a book by Eakins and Eakins called Sex Differences in Human Communication.

The Eakinses point out that the larynx or voice box of the adult male (its projection at the front of the throat is commonly called the Adam's Apple) is generally larger than the female's.

Small tough bands of connective tissue in the larynx form the vocal cords. During speech these vibrate when we force breath from our lungs to produce vocal tones for the voice sound. Most men have longer and thicker vocal bands than most women. The greater the number of times the vocal cords vibrate, the higher the sound we subjectively hear as pitch . . . since most adult males have larger and thicker vocal cords than the majority of women do, men's voices tend to be lower in pitch. Females usually have higher-pitched voices than males because their vocal bands are shorter and thinner. Their voices are about two-thirds of an octave higher than the pitch levels of men's voices.

The pitch of the vocal cords is probably not the only clue that tells us whether a voice is male or female. The vocal tract, through which the vibrating sound must pass, is that air-filled tube divided by the lips, tongue, soft palate and the cavities— of the mouth, nose, larynx and throat. These cavities are like echo chambers, and they reinforce or build up the loudness of tones.

Stylistic Differences

Despite these physiological differences there is still variation in the way men and women talk, variation that must be considered stylistic as it develops according to linguistic custom. According to the Eakinses: Men and women may modify the sounds they produce to make them conform to male and female archetypes. In other words, men tend to talk as though they were bigger and women as though they were smaller than they actually may be.

The pitch of voices is created not only by physical differences, but by cultural pressure and stereotypes.

Our culture tends to make mock of high voices. The best case (or perhaps the worst) is a falsetto. Have you ever tried to talk in falsetto or have you heard a "T" talking in a falsetto that she thought sounded feminine? Quite the opposite effect, isn't it? A falsetto is simply too high, particularly in a culture that seems to admire low-pitched women's voices that are slightly breathy in quality.

Whatever the natural pitch of your voice, you really can do something to change it. The Eakinses have a system that uses a piano to locate the habitual pitch, or level, at which each of their students normally speak. They then determine the level at which a person can produce vocal tones most efficiently and most comfortably, tones with good quality and loudness. The Eakinses conclude with the "general rule of thumb that optimum or natural pitch is probably one-fourth to one-third above the lowest levels of an individual's total pitch range."

My vocal coach uses a variation of this same system. She first teaches "T"s (and others) to breathe from the diaphragm. (Most men and women speak from the throat or upper chest). That seems like a very simple statement—but it's one that most individuals, "T"s or not, simply do not understand. As a result, most people don't support their voices with enough breath. By breathing through your diaphragm you can take in, and hence expel, much more air. This gives you voice control—over pitch, total quality, volume, inflection and projection. It is the foundation for good speaking ability and good vocal health.

My vocal teacher further suggests that I hum to the highest pitch at which I am comfortable in order to determine a pitch that I can use in my day to day talking. So I begin to hum, going higher and higher up the scale as far as I can go without hitting a falsetto. She then suggests that I try to talk in that high voice. I found that it was very difficult to do, very unnatural. Even getting through one or two sentences was a strain.

She then recommends that I hum up to that high point, this time going back down the scale a note or two until I can control the sound with relative ease. She has me begin to try talking in that voice.

I soon found out that with practice, I could find a comfortable voice level, both psychologically and physically, —one that didn't put a constant strain on my voice, yet one that was much higher than my naturally lower, "male" voice. The voice I ended up with, the one which I use as a woman, seems very natural and very comfortable and it puts absolutely no strain on my vocal chords. As posed by the Eakinses and borne out of my own experience, it soon becomes habitual to speak in the higher feminine voice. It is a perfectly natural way for me to speak and I consider it my own feminine voice. In no way do I feel that I am pretending to be someone I'm not. Indeed, when reverting back to my male voice I find that it takes a conscious effort to lower my voice. The first time this happened I came to the realization that either of those two voices was actually "me."

Incidentally, early in the morning and sometimes after talking for long periods of time your voice may come out sounding much lower than you might expect or desire. I find myself practicing the higher pitch in the mornings in order not to slip. This can be outright embarrassing.

Intonation

Our voices don't always stay at one level, do they?

The changes in pitch that occur when we speak are termed intonation.

There is no question about the fact that males and females intone their speech differently and that they convey a different message with their intonation.

Intonation, say the Eakinses, is something like a musical melody that is spoken but not sung. When the

voice shifts from one definite pitch to another with a break, generally between the syllables of the word or between words, this is called a step. Pitch changes that are continuous and occur without breaks in flow are termed inflections. These pitch variations may be rapid or slow, rising, falling, or circumplex (combinations of rising-falling, falling-rising patterns).

Here's the good news for "T"s. Studies show that the average pitch level of an individual's voice may be less important to overall effectiveness in communicating masculinity or femininity than variations in pitch.

In other words, using a greater range of inflections can give you a much more feminine-sounding voice.

No doubt about it, certain intonation characteristics may be identifiable by sex. Women supposedly speak in an overall high pitch, and women are said to use the highest pitch level more than men and in general to speak with more expressive intonation patterns.

Volume

By and large, men speak more loudly than women.

While little research has been done on the subject, male speakers in general talk with greater intensity than females.

Particularly when females are speaking to someone of the same sex, female to female, they speak more softly. When females speak to males, they increase their intensity. Researchers interpret this to mean that subjects probably feel a greater affiliation with a person of the same sex than with one of the opposite sex.

In our culture the voice of authority tends to be a loud one. Weak voices indicate timid personalities or an extreme reaction to a speaking situation. In fact, many women who see themselves in submissive or nonauthoritarian roles seem to reflect these self-perceptions in their voices.

My own voice teacher is constantly nagging at me to speak louder. Her system is to get me to look directly at the person to whom I am speaking, and to speak to that person, no other. She feels that in directing my speech I will enunciate properly and use the right pitch, yet still achieve sufficient loudness or timbre to be able to get the message across.

I try to remember not to speak as loudly as when I lived as a man, particularly in public situations where a loud voice at any pitch might draw attention that I really don't want. (If you really want attention, speak up!)

Too loud or too soft? You'll have to find out for yourself through lots of practice. Generally, soft- spoken women are more acceptable in today's society than loud mouths, especially particularly low-pitched loud mouths.

Womentalk

Some elements of women's speech differ radically from men's speech.

That doesn't mean that women's speech is generally bad or inferior and men's good and superior; it simply means that women, in addition to varying their intonation of words, use a number of communication techniques which offer an alternative to those used by men.

The "tag question" is a good example of conversational technique used by women. Most speech therapists believe that it's used by women to avoid making strong statements. What is a tag question? "Mary is going tomorrow . . . isn't she?"

The tag question lies somewhere between a statement and a question. It is less assertive than an outright statement and it is useful in a situation where an outright statement might not be appropriate and where a yes/no question is not fitting.

Tag questions are used to confirm something you suspect to be true. They "tag" a partial question to the end of a statement.

Tag questions are also used by women in social situations. "Sure is fun here, isn't it?" might be a question asked by a woman at a party as an icebreaker. Men might simply state "Sure is fun in here" without the tag at the end.

Another tag question is often used by women seeking confirmation or commitment. Your daughter might ask you, for example, "I can have the car tonight, can't I"?

This pattern of opinion giving, followed by a tag question, is allegedly more common among women than men. In fact, women's speech in general is said to be more polite than men's speech. The tag question is simply a convention of polite speech.

Qualifiers

Women's language also contains an abundance of qualifiers—words that soften, mitigate, or qualify phrases in other words.

Qualifiers seem to make our words less absolute in tone. Words such as a "well, let's see, perhaps, possibly, I suppose, I think, it seems to me, you know" and words of that ilk are considered qualifiers.

Counterbalancing the directness and force of a statement by adding qualifiers will make the speech sound more tentative.

Other qualifiers or softeners are words such as "rather, somewhat, sort of, to some extent."

Disclaimers are another form of qualifiers. Disclaimers are usually introductory expressions that excuse, explain or request understanding or forbearance, such as "I may be wrong but . . ." or "You may not like this, but . . ." or "I know this sounds silly, but I think . . ."

Women often end a sentence with a question or by inflecting the last word.

This is one of the most difficult things for "T"s to learn because it represents a whole new way of speaking.

Bringing the voice up at the end of a sentence softens the sentence, putting the "T" in a position of appearing to question her own statements. That little bit of expressed insecurity, a feeling in the listener that the "T" needs an answer, is considered very feminine.

Women also articulate more carefully; they have a greater range and frequency of inflection than men.

If you were going to chart the way that most men talk you could draw a straight line across each word of a sentence. In contrast, if you charted a women's vocal presentation the lines representing their words would go up and down more dramatically. Women have greater range in their talk as well as greater inflection.

There is also a feminine vocabulary.

Words such as "gorgeous," "lovely," and "precious" are the types of words commonly heard in everyday womantalk, words that most heterosexual men never use.

Some techniques for developing "proper" language can be learned through observation and rehearsal. For example, saying "housecoat" rather than "robe" would take a bit of learning for most men just beginning their transition toward a more feminine vocabulary.

It takes time to build a new vocabu-lary, but using new words until they become a natural part of everyday usage can be an important move towards a more acceptable feminine presentation with voice.

There is definitely a language of gender. Women put much more emphasis on adjectives and adverbs than men.

A woman might say "That's _so_ beautiful" where a man might say "That's _so_ _beautiful_." Learning to put emphasis and inflection on certain words is a time-consuming but necessary step for any "T".

The pronunciation of words, genderized or not, can also have a feminizing effect.

For example, if you can learn to say your "s's" almost as if you were hissing like a snake, you'll find that you will have a more feminine presentation.

Women tend to use their "t"s, particularly at the end of a sentence, in a much softer manner than most men. After a while this can come almost automatically; but practicing words with some s's and t's in front of a mirror or into a recorder can be a great help.

The Eakinses admit that it's dangerous to conclude that there are fixed rules which govern women's and men's styles of speech. In general, they make the two observations which follow, observations which summarize the conclusions of present research.

1) Women's speech tends to be more person- centered and concerned with interpersonal matters. It is apt to deal with the speaker's own and other's feelings. It is more polite, more indirect, and uses the method of implication. It employs qualifiers and other softening devices to avoid

imposing belief, agreement, or obedience on others through overly strong statements, questions or commands.

2)Men's speech tends to be more centered around external things and is more apt to involve straight factual communication. It is more literal, direct, and to the point. It employs stronger statements and forms that tend to press compliance, agreement, or a belief on the listener.

There is a definite linguistic "double standard" in the existence of typical male and female speech styles.

In their excellent book Language and the Sexes, Frank and Anshen say:

An example of speech which has traditionally been considered more "masculine" and less proper is the use of obscenities. In a study among Long Island college students, Anshen found that male students were twice as likely as female students to use obscenities, although there was little difference in the strength of the obscenities that were used by the two sexes. Interestingly, though, while men made a clear effort to "clean up" their speech in the presence of women, no similar effect was noticed for women in mixed company. Although they still used obscenities less often than did men, their usage did not seem at all inhibited by the presence of men.

On a personal note, I find that my own language is much less obscene as a woman than it was when I lived as a full-time man. It seems that I find myself thinking about what I am saying more, and concluding that to use obscenities as a woman would be alien to the refined front I am trying to present. Even the occasional "damn" or "hell" comes difficult to my lips as a woman. Come to think of it, I'm probably a better person for it, too. One more benefit of "T"ism.

The body and the voice
As we've said throughout this book, women smile more than men.

Facial movements, especially during speech, can add to your feminine presentation.

Why do women smile more than men?

It's not that they're necessarily happy or amused. In fact, the smile may be an indicator of traditional social status, used as a gesture of cultural submission.

Supposedly, the smile is an indicator of submission, particularly of women to men.

When a woman and a man talk, particularly if they're only moderately well acquainted, the smile (rather than indicating friendliness or pleasure) supposedly shows that no aggression or harm is intended.

Perhaps women smile more to cover up uneasiness or nervousness about meeting social expectations.

Whatever the psychological reason behind the smile, accept the fact that women smile more than men. Smiling while you are talking will elicit a response from most listeners. Because you'll need all the help you can get, keep on smiling!

When women talk they move their mouths more than men; here again, smiling comes into play. If you don't believe it, try talking while smiling and talking without smiling. It's much easier to talk with a smile. Your mouth moves more, you're more animated and people tend to have a warmer feeling as they listen to you.

There's a sharp difference in eye contact according to sex, too. Women look more at the person to whom they're speaking than men do. Women look at one another more and hold eye contact longer with each other than men do with other men. The usual explanation given for this phenomenon is that women are more willing to establish and maintain eye contact because they are more inclined towards social and interpersonal relations. Perhaps the gaze is an avenue of emotional expression for women. The more positive the attitude towards the person being addressed, the more eye contact there will be.

People tend to do more looking while they are listening to another speaker than when they themselves are speaking, and women are listeners more often than talkers. Perhaps you've become a much better listener in the feminine role, particularly if you look at who is doing the talking.

Women are much more prone to reveal their emotions than men. The theory is that men are "internalizers," that they keep their emotions inside. Women, on the other hand, allow their feelings to show more frequently.

For whatever reason, the more facial expression, the more smiles, the more you can look and listen, the better the feminine conversationalist you will be. Good advice for all of us, isn't it?

Women tend to use their hands in expressing themselves much more than men do.

Watch women talk. Watch their hands and how often they are used. Hands come to the chest, they point, they are used in flowing and demonstrative ways to "say" exactly what the speaker means.

Very often the wrist is dropped and raised with the fingers kept together. This small gesture creates a very feminine look, complementing and entrancing the femininity of the voice.

Some general thoughts

Nothing is a bigger giveaway than coughing or clearing your throat in a low voice. Often, in a moment of physical necessity, "T"s cough or loudly blow their noses, giving their gender away.

It takes practice to clear your throat or cough in a high voice, but it becomes automatic. A practical "T" would no more cough or clear her throat in a low voice than she would talk in one. It's as simple as that, if you practice.

Remember gender attribution. People believe what they see.

You won't have any trouble with your presentation, (or with your voice) if you approach the viewer/listener from a distance, let the attribution be made and begin to talk in your feminine voice.

The attribution has already been made—they've made a judgment about you and already believe that you are a woman. Then when they hear you talk in almost any kind of soft voice, even at a lower pitch than the average woman, they'll still believe it's a simply a lower-pitched woman's voice.

Conversely, when you begin to talk in a low voice and you're behind somebody, you surprise them. They haven't yet had a chance to make a judgment about who you are. You open yourself up for a situation that might be embarrassing; in short, you open yourself up to be read.

Again with practice this will happen automatically. You let people see you, allowing them to make a judgment about who you are with their eyes instead of their ears alone. This is particularly important if you are at all uncomfortable about your voice.

The acid test for your feminine voice is the telephone.

There's something about a phone that filters out the feminine; try as you might, the masculine voice comes through.

A booklet published by the Erikson Educational Foundation, full of advice for transsexuals on passing techniques, offers the following helpful hint: "When introducing yourself on the telephone, begin the conversation by saying, 'This is Miss X.' In that way, should you still need some practice in feminizing your voice, and if the person on the other end of the line is in some doubt as to your sex, this assertion usually will resolve the question in your favor."

Once again, the one point we've made repeatedly throughout this book bears repeating. Once a gender attribution is made, the particulars (in this case the voice) will be filtered through that attribution and used to confirm it.

Hormones and the voice

As tempting as it is to believe it, hormones do not change the voice or feminize it.

It would be easy for those who plan to go far on the "T" spectrum to believe that hormones will help soften the voice, bring the pitch higher and make the intonation more feminine.

It simply doesn't work that way. There are no short- cuts to developing a more feminized voice.

Surgery

Another no-no is attempting to alter your voice through surgery.

Yes, I know that some doctors suggest an operation to shorten the larynx.

And, yes, I've known some "T"s who've had this operation, hoping against hope to feminize their voices.

But I have never known a "T", never, who had a voice operation that was successful. There may be some, but it is an experiment that might help doctors get rich at your expense.

If you're even considering an operation on your voice, talk to a number of "T"s, particularly post-operative "T"s, to find out exactly what they did with their voices.

Should you find someone who has had a successful operation, get additional recommendations from other "T"s who have used that same doctor.

By and large, you're generally a lot better off not having a voice operation. Too many things can go wrong; there are very few that can go right.

Professional help

One of the best investments you can make is to hire a voice teacher.

Every community has voice teachers. Some are better than others, of course, but voice teachers, even drama teachers, can help you feminize your own voice better than you could ever do it yourself.

Your local college, even the yellow pages of the phone book, will list available voice teachers. You'll certainly be able to find one who is understanding, one who can differentiate the nuances involved in feminizing the voice and who can work with you on the language, intonation, and other facets of creating a more feminine voice.

Even if a voice teacher has never taught a "T" before, he or she will be happy to have you . . .and your money. A voice teacher will help you develop proper pitch, timbre, resonance, and word pronunciation.

You won't need a lot of visits either, particularly if you have or can get a tape recorder. Once you understand the basics in feminizing your voice, a tape recorder is a magic tool. It allows you to tape yourself and listen to yourself, and to make changes accordingly. Simply knowing what to listen for is a tremendous help in voice feminization.

Practical tips

I've always found it's helpful to tape my male voice and then my "T" voice, then compare the two. It's amazing the difference you can create, if you work for it.

You can also practice by talking back to the radio. Listen to your car radio, tuning to a woman speaking. After she says a sentence, you repeat it. Try to say it in the same voice, the same timbre, as she does. Practice makes perfect and the radio gives you a good opportunity to do just that.

The best advice on voice is that you practice. You should practice, practice, and then practice some more. Practice with cassette tapes, radio, and in person.

Non-"T"s change their voices; so can you. If you control your voice, you can begin to control your life.

You really can change. Your voice reflects the music in your soul. You're willing to change everything else. Changing your voice is simply a matter of making a decision to do so and then working on it.

Finally, remember that as a child you imitated someone's voice. That imitation became your voice, it became "you." But what is "you"? It's the voice you want to have, the voice people hear. It's a projection you make.

As soon as you get used to your feminized voice, talking in any other voice will sound strange to you. In fact, you soon reach a point where you simply cannot talk in any way other than a feminine manner when you are dressed, when you are projecting your feminine self.

So listen, observe other women, get a professional voice teacher and then practice, practice, practice.

Now.

Chapter 7

Hormones

If there were a magic pill . . .
a lot of "T"s would term it "hormones."

There isn't a magic pill, of course. Nothing will turn the male body into a 100% female body even over a long period of time.

"T"s have flights of fantasy. At one time or another, we all believe that female hormones are the answer to our dreams of achieving a more feminized body. Basically, the dream <u>can</u> be realized in many cases if hormones, under supervision, are used properly along with ample doses of study, good judgment and careful planning. The degree of change using hormones will differ for every person. Know in advance that the degree of change is not predictable.

The risk factor in taking hormones has to be weighed against the present quality of your life. You'll have to judge how treatment will affect your "T" expectations, even your expectations regarding life itself.

You'll have to carefully judge the pros and cons about taking pills or injections. There is no way around it.

Hopefully, this chapter will give you a foundation on which to build your eventual decision to begin or not to begin the female hormone procedure.

<u>What are hormones, anyway?</u>
Hormones are complex chemical structures which are manufactured in very small amounts by special organs of the body.

When hormones are secreted directly into the bloodstream and carried to an end organ, they will have an effect upon that end organ which may produce a specific result or reaction.

The hormones that are of most interest to "T"s are estrogens, progesterones, and androgens:
1) Estrogens are produced naturally by females and are secreted by the ovary,

the adrenal, and by the tissues of pregnancy. Twenty-two separate estrogens have been isolated.

2) Progesterones are produced naturally by females. Their main purpose is in preparing the lining of the uterus to receive the fertilized egg. They also act to feminize the body fat distribution (breasts/hip development). They may cause lactation, the regulation of the monthly menstrual cycle, and affect such psychological matters as libido and depression. When women have PMS—Premenstrual Syndrome—they are basically dealing with the effect that progesterones have on their bodies.

3) Androgens are produced naturally by males in the form of testosterone. They are secreted by the testes, and to a lesser extent by the adrenal glands. Androgens cause pubertal development of the testes, production of facial and body hair, the lowering of the voice, and other "male" oriented physical attributes.

All three hormones are produced by both genders.

What exactly do these hormones do in the female body?

In general, they reflect the overall growth and development of the human female and the monthly cyclical process which makes the female fertile on a regular basis. Hormones are responsible for the blood vessel integrity and the external appearance of that same body—skin, hair texture, and distribution. They are also cardioprotective-they help your heart.

Effects of hormones

What happens to your body may not happen to mine, and vice versa.

The sensitivity of any tissue reaction to a given hormone dosage, and consequently, the degree of change, is different for different individuals.

In general terms, here are the changes that can be expected as a result of a regulated hormone plan:

1)Breasts: Both estradiol and progesterone have effects upon the breasts. The estrogen influences the glandular portion, the progesterone influences the ductal system or skeleton which holds the glandular tissue in place.

Breasts may become sore, a sign that they are undergoing change.

Breast enlargements start as a thickening of the bud of glandular tissue present behind the pigmented area around the nipple. The main enlargement takes the form of increased fat and water deposits behind this "plate" or breast mass. There may be a deepening of the pigmentation of the nipple and areola, and a degree of enlargement to the nipple. There may also be a small secretion from the nipple. Increased fat level may produce quite respectable breasts, but growth does vary with the individual. Breast mass in "T"s is usually more dense than that of genetic females. During hormone treatment, some doctors recommend that "T"'s use a special breast pump in order to increase the size of the nipple and the areola. Again, results will vary with the individual, the application of the cup, the effect of the hormones, and the dedication of the "T."

"T"s seem to expect overnight miracles but this simply does not happen. Breast development takes months to occur, depending on age, degree of body fat and other physical differences. Age is another important factor. For someone in their early 20's, female hormones will have a much quicker and more positive effect than for someone, say, in their 40's or 50's. This is due to the number of years that testosterone has had to affect the metabolism.

Remember: taking estrogens in large doses will not necessarily cause breasts to grow as large as you might want. Large doses won't cause them to grow as quickly as you might hope, either. Breast development potential is determined by genetics. If your mother, sister or other close blood relatives are small-breasted, you will likely be small-breasted as well. Having well-endowed blood relatives does not guarantee "adequate" breast development. In any event, women's bodies develop breasts over a period of a few years. You cannot expect your body to change any quicker than that.

Be aware of the possibility of sudden growth spurts in the size of your breasts. There are many cases of impatient people opting for silicone breast implants after a few months on estrogens, only to have their natural breasts suddenly develop, leaving them with overly large breasts. These, in turn, cause the same discomfort and backaches as they would for any other woman.

2) Body contours: Those on hormones may find a small increase in hip circumference, in the circumference of the thighs, and in the pads of fat typical to the female on the side of the neck, back of the shoulder and upper arms.

The sharp outlines of the face may be softened by "filling out" with an infiltration of fat that arises from hormone intake. Caution—it's an unfortunate fact that diet-ing sometimes results in a loss of the fat from the breasts while the breast tissue remains in place.

3) Skin: Hormones help retard the ageing process of the skin. The skin will soften, will become smoother, silkier, translucent, elastic . . . and sensitive.

4) Hair: Blood supply to the skin will increase so there is sometimes an improvement of head hair. A lot of this depends on your own genetic inheritance . . . if you are bald or getting bald, hormones alone won't do a great deal to give you a new head of hair. Body hair may assume a female pattern of density. Don't expect your beard growth to stop just because you are taking female hormones. The jury is still out on this one, but the consensus is that if electrology is undertaken regularly, hair growth may be retarded if associated with estrogen doses.

Many "T"s taking hormones have told me that because of the softer skin, electrolysis is more painful than the work they had done prior to beginning the hormonal treatment. But the good news is that hair apparently comes out easier for those on hormones. Whether this is scientifically correct is anyone's guess—but emotions, as you will see below, do play an important part in hormonal treatment and in the "T" movement in general.

5) Genitalia: The testes will probably decrease in size, but hormones will not make your penis atrophy. It may appear to do so, for in the long run, estrogens cause "chemical castration," i.e. impotence and sterility.

6) <u>Voice</u>: No magic here. Hormone treatment does not change the voice of males to females in any way.

7) <u>Psychological effects</u>: We've mentioned the decrease of libido (your sexual drive). I have never met a "T" on hormones who has not commented about this fact.

There may also be a change in mood and a reversal of certain aggressive tendencies. Perhaps this is an emotional effect, not so much due to hormonal reaction but rather to psychic adjustment.

It is not unusual for hormones to cause an emotional cycle with ups and downs. Weepiness, indecisiveness and passivity or placidity are not uncommon symptoms for those who take hormones.

Hormones are not magic pills. They aren't miracle drugs and they can't turn a man into a woman overnight or ever.

Estrogens will bring out dormant feminine potential in a male. Taken before the operation, however, they are always fighting the male hormone (androgens), which they may help to override but not eliminate.

Remember that as a genetic-born male taking estrogens, there are a number of other potential problems to consider. Your ability to have sex as a male will be greatly reduced or eliminated. This includes masturbation. If you do engage in sex, even occasionally, you'll find that your penis may be very tender and that erections have become painful. The relatively sudden loss of sexual function as a male may cause prostate infections with symptoms very similar to many venereal diseases (discharge, backache, painful urination, etc.).

8) <u>Side effects</u>: As Dr. Sheila Kirk, well-known "T" and hormone expert has said:

Keep in mind that with each medicine or drug—each pharmaceutical chemical, whether it be for your heart or digestion, whether it be to induce sleep or keep you awake, to treat an infection or eliminate pain—there are reactions or side effects other than what is intended primarily in the mode of action of the substance.

Dr. Kirk goes on to list the possible problems with estrogen and progesterone therapy, including gall bladder disease, thrombotic disorders, hypertension, fluid retention, psychiatric disorders, jaundice, skin disease, and a host of other problems.

But Dr. Kirk also adds,

This is quite a formidable list and at first—frightening! But it need not be! Good evaluative procedures when undertaken and evaluated will show that most people are quite safe in using these medications and will continue to use them comfortably as well as effectively.

Many "T"s have told us that taking estrogen has caused a number of physical problems. Remember that estrogen preparations are gastric irritants. Often there is nausea, vomiting, diarrhea or other changes in bowel habits. For this reason, estrogen is normally taken with food. Fortunately, the ill feeling often passes after some weeks of taking the drug.

A side effect that is not too difficult to live with is nail brittleness. The absorption and metabolism of vitamins is affected by the hormone treatment, so nails become brittle and crack easily. However, multi-vitamin preparations and some oils can help with this problem.

Doctors suggest that people with a history of heart disease, abnormal liver functioning, diabetes and other pancreas disorders, cancer, and pituitary gland tumors not take the female hormones.

Every doctor I know who has dealt with hormones for "T"s strongly urges the "T" to ask for regular blood pressure checks and blood lipids tests, particularly for early detection of any thrombalembolic disorder (blood clot forming, specifically a stroke, deep vein thrombosis, pulmonary embolism and myocardial infarction). Doctors also suggest that an annual chemistry panel, including liver and blood lipids as well as hormone levels, be taken by anyone on a regular regimen of hormones.

Getting started

Rule number one when starting on hormones is to understand what you must do to ensure your continuing health.

This, of course, means a complete medical evaluation by a qualified physician.

Where to find a doctor who understands and is sympathetic to the "T" phenomenon is not something I can address here. You can ask another "T" or a support group for the names of qualified doctors in your area.

Qualified doctors will take a complete history, and perform a complete medical evaluation on you which includes a family and personal history of disease and illness. Paramount to the success of the hormonal treatment will be a complete review of all past health problems as they relate to your heart, any blood vessel disease and past use of street hormones.

The doctor will probably give you laboratory studies which should include a blood profile and an electrocardiogram as well as treadmill studies. The doctor will also look for any history of liver or kidney disease and any problems with metabolic disease, particularly with calcium and phosphorous imbalances.

He or she will make sure that you aren't a diabetic or pre-diabetic and that you have no hint of cholesterol abnormalities. The doctor will look for possible thyroid disease, check the vein competency in your legs and pelvic areas and conduct any other special tests needed as indicated by your history. Together, you and your doctor will weigh the risks of hormones against the benefits. In most cases, it will be possible to go forward, but only under close medical supervision.

In short, using the services of a qualified physician is an absolute must; it's the only way to take hormones. Any physician who takes a short-cut or who does not find out about your personal and famly history is, to say the least, questionable.

A qualified doctor will make you a partner in your own health care. Your final decision on hormone therapy is going to be up to you. That decision can only be made on the basis of full knowledge concerning what you can and can't expect from medication on three levels: physical, psychological and emotional.

As a person taking hormones, you

must be aware of the risks and their early warning signals. Accurate expectations of the various kinds of changes you can expect are a must. You would do well to know what will not be affected by hormone therapy.

As a partner in this process, you will also need to know that the complicated monitoring involved is essential to your future health.

You will certainly come to an understanding that abuse of the medication can result in many problems, including serious illness and in some cases, death. Abuse of hormones coupled with substance abuse (such as alcohol or drugs) can have horrible consequences. Hormones are not a benign or recreational medication, and their misuse without proper supervision can produce critical results.

Standards of Care

Tommye Kelley, MA (a Denver psychotherapist working primarily with gender-conflicted persons, crossdressers, and their significant others) submitted an essay to the International Foundation for Gender Education on the Standards of Care for hormone therapy.

The Standards of Care she discusses in that essay are the qualifications a transsexual must meet prior to eventual surgery, a list developed by experts on the founding committee on the Harry Benjamin International Gender Dysphoria Association which is reprinted in the appendix of this book.

Noting that the Standards of Care require only 90 days of psychotherapy prior to beginning a course of hormones, Ms. Kelley describes the Standards as a barebones guide, minimum requirements that should not be undercut. She states in her essay that the Standards do not dictate a fixed schedule, and she stresses that what needs to be done can be done. She continues:

There are several things that must be explored and resolution begun before any consideration of hormones. This is not a situation of entitlement, nor is it a situation of self diagnosis and self determination. Hormones are not a benign medication; this medication carries all sorts of possible complications, beginning with the very real possibility of creating a "pseudo transsexual" by hormonally feminizing a genetic male who may only be cycling up or over-reacting to a temporary situation in his life.

EVALUATION AND DIAGNOSIS:

This is a process that cannot be rushed, as in-depth case history is essential. Observation of the client over time is an aid to this procedure. It is not enough for a sincere and well-meaning client to come into the office and emotionally insist that he has felt like a woman all his life, or that he is not a "transsexual" but a "woman". The client is paying the clinician to be stronger and more objective than he can be himself. The client is paying for the therapist to spend her time and energy in studying and researching this subject, in fact, to have more information and awareness than he can have. It is through this information and objectivity that evaluation must come.

The client needs to explore in depth his experience in relationships, especially love relationships. He needs to be freshly aware of the attitudes and expectations that he took into those relationships and how well those attitudes and expectations worked. He needs to look at what he got from the relationship and how he will deal with the changes that hormone therapy will bring about. If he is in a marital relationship, that must be resolved before hormones. The marriage contract implies sexual activity. Taking estrogen will interfere with such activity, if not make it entirely impossible. It is unethical to provide an extraneous medication that is deliberately calculated to interfere with one's ability to fulfill the implied contract. Simply for a spouse to come into the office and state that it is all right with her for her husband to take estrogen is not enough. It is the responsibility of the therapist to see some reasonable resolution between the primary client and the relationship partner before hormones are administered. If the therapist cannot see resolution in which she feels comfortable, it is inappropriate to prescribe hormones.

If the primary client is not ready to resolve the relationship, then he is not ready to make the ultimate sacrifices for his "womanhood". This gives the therapeutic relationship a luxury of time in which the client and the therapist can further explore other explanations for his feelings of gender conflict. Such an event should not be viewed as a failure or a difficulty. It is an advantage and may be the most important element of recovery or discovery for the client. (After all, the therapeutic goal should be finding out what is necessary for the client.)

The therapeutic process needs to focus on the client's attitude toward his genitals. Both the therapist and client must keep in mind that the medication under consideration is (possibly) going to render his genitals flaccid and nonfunctional. Even masturbation may become difficult or nearly impossible. What has the attitude toward the genitals been over time? What are the ways in which this attitude has been demonstrated? What time period are we talking about?

During the first 90 days the therapist needs to listen closely for self-reports of cyclical feelings in the compulsive behaviors and feelings. It is the intensity of the feelings and thought processes on which these observations need to focus, not the frequency. In exploring the episodes from the past when the client sought, or considered seeking help with the dressing or gender problem, when suicide was attempted or seriously considered, a cyclic pattern of thoughts and feelings emerge. When the client can be made aware of such a pattern in his own self-report and encouraged to examine this pattern in order to more clearly chart its course, he may well be able to see that what has occurred in the past may very well reoccur in his life although at the moment that feels quite improbable. A full familiarity with the nature of cycling is essential prior to any consideration of hormones.

Stopping

If you are serious about sexual reassignment, don't start taking hormones if you have even the most fleeting thought about stopping.

It's easy advice to give, hard to take. But stopping hormones, reregulating your body back to where it was when you were manufacturing testosterone, simply isn't that easy. Infertility is one possible outcome, depending on the dosage levels of female hormones and the length of time during which they're taken.

Mood swings and readjusting to the withdrawal of female hormones may add to the psychological problems that need to be resolved.

There are apparent physical problems that need taking care of, too. For example, after your body is conditioned to receiving female hormones, it will take time to resume production of its own hormones again. During this period, the reduction or lack of hormones necessary for functioning might be felt acutely as depression, lethargy and irritability.

With the return of testosterone, you could experience sudden intense periods of aggression, belligerence and driven compulsions that characterize male reality. These symptoms will pose extreme difficulties for you and the people around you—in essence, your system will be stripped of the control and coping mechanisms it learned during adolescence. These behaviors and emotions make withdrawal from hormones as difficult as any other drug withdrawal. Hormones are addictive.

Physical problems including enlarged breasts must also be dealt with. Some breasts revert to their original appearance when estrogen is withdrawn, depending on when it is stopped and on how much actual breast tissue has grown. Some don't. Depending on the size of the breasts, it may be necessary to have a mastectomy performed. Mastectomies aren't easy in the best of circumstances. They are even more difficult for "T"s because of the embarrassment the operation may entail and the future scars that will show.

Conclusion

Taking hormones sounds scary, doesn't it?

It can be frightening, but most individuals are medically cleared to take hormones and do it quite safely.

You'll be weighing the risk factor against the present quality of your life. That's why you'll have to weigh the potential of the benefits against the possibility of the consequences.

You will be evaluating your overall expectations regarding life itself, no small task.

You'll have to be patient and careful.

You'll monitor what is happening, you'll continue to work with your physician.

But for those "T"s who have gone through a complete course of hormonal therapy and who continue to use hormones, the result seems to be well worth the effort.

Finally, there are some do's and don'ts for the use of hormones, guidelines compiled by the Self-help Association for Transsexuals in South Ascot, England. These suggestions serve as our final words on the subject of hormones.

SUMMARY

Some "DO'S" and "DON'TS" for the use of hormones:

DO go to a doctor or Gender Identity Center to get hormones

DON'T   try to get them from other "T"s—they may not be the right ones for you.

DO take them regularly once you have them. Large gaps in your regimen will curtail your development. Therefore be sure of yourself and what you really want before you start.

DO try to have a thorough medical examination prior to taking hormones, paying particular attention to cardiac history and problems, blood pressure and circulatory efficiency. General practitioners are very lax about this, unless you ask.

DO take the initially prescribed dosage, which may be less than the average quoted earlier. This is especially important to begin with. There is nothing to be gained, and much harm may be done, by going 'over the top'.

DON'T have unrealistic expectations. There will be some body changes but they will not appear overnight, (6 months to 2 years is the normal range of time) nor will they be very dramatic. For example, it is probably the minority of M to F TSs who develop enough breast growth not to need implants.

DO stop taking hormones prior to gender reassignment surgery, whatever your surgeon does or does not say! All medication should cease before any surgical operation. This is especially important for M to F TSs where estrogen dosage increases the risk of blood clotting.

DO reduce the level of dosage after the operation. DON'T cut it out altogether—the body needs a maintenance hormone balance—but remember that too much is unnecessary and could be dangerous.

DO try and have regular blood pressure and blood lipids tests (at least once a year) after the operation. Again, you may have to specially request your GP to refer you to a hospital for the latter.

Finally, DON'T be paranoid or fanatical about hormones! Use them well and they will eventually satisfy you.

Chapter 8

Significant Others

"On Disclosure"
To my dear friends and fellow
lovers of grouped words
Assembled there and then
for purposes direct and circumspect.
Curious and expectant, kindly
and supporting
Eager and reluctant, wishful
and bashful, prideful and effacing
I give you then and now
ourselves.
A study in our strengths,
weaknesses, joys and sorrows
And our attempts at
communication and the awful,
awesome spectre of the intimate
self-revelation of our innermost
beingness.
Our totems, our stigmata some
acceptable, some not we think -
Dare we? Might we?

What will "They" think or feel,
or judge, or do.
If we masquers doff our masks
of painful self-protection and cop to
our hiddenmost internal feelings,
truths, knowings?
Would you, could they can I,
Accept us as we are?
Where lie the bounds of
Propriety and good sense?
If that is the term?
Where lie the frontiers of
friendship of loving, of caring,
Or is it all simply ego tripping,
Wish fulfilling fantasy?
Would you, could they, can I
Accept yourself or them, or me
If we all but knew The Truth?
by Jacqueline

—in Tapestry magazine

89

"T"ism is a great compromise.

The vast majority of "T"s would like to practice their "hobby" much more often than they do.

Economic circumstances and time restraints, but more importantly, family situations, usually dictate the amount of time, money and energy a "T" can devote to her activities.

Most "T"s live with what I call the "great compromise," a compromise with themselves.

This compromise involves the subversion and repression of feelings about "T"ism in hopes of preserving a marriage, keeping a family together or maintaining some other significant personal relationship, including those with parents.

It is the rare "T", indeed, who is comfortable enough with herself to be able to share her desire to spend time, or actually "become" a woman with family and friends, be they wives, children, parents, coworkers, or close friends.

Yet as "T"s grow older, they realize that their true selves are locked in and cutoff, never or at best rarely shared with others. Consequently, many "T"s live only partial lives, never experiencing themselves or realizing their full potential as "whole" persons.

Somewhere along the road the maturing "T" begins to understand that she has been living her life for others . . . not so much for herself. As the awareness of mortality approaches (this usually happens in the late 30s or early 40s), "T"s begin to understand that there is only a limited amount of time left to live life for themselves.

It is at this point in their lives that "T"s literally start to come out of the closet, both socially and with their families. They decide that their previously repressed feminine selves are vitally important to the expression of total self. They begin to understand that they must live life to the fullest for themselves, and that expressing their feelings is an absolute necessity.

"Living a lie," living in the closet, in fact, life in general becomes intolerable. Sneaking around and lying to mates, family and friends becomes unacceptable. When "T"s can no longer live with their secret, significant others are told, often without the benefit of careful preparation.

Many relationships break down at this point. The guilt associated with being a "T", coupled with a lack of support and guidance, often overrides common sense, splitting the family unit asunder.

Professional help

It may be too late for most "T"s reading these words, but every "T" should seek and contract professional help prior to making the great revelation to family or significant other.

Having said this, we understand well that most helping professionals (therapists, psychologists, social workers and psychiatrists) know relatively little about the "T" phenomenon.

In fact, most "T"s who seek professional help spend much of their early therapy educating the professional. As a rule, most therapists and other professionals don't see "T"s on a daily basis. Chances are that the average therapist will come into contact with only one or two during a lifetime, which makes the pursuit of professional help a precarious proposition for the "T" in need of counsel and support.

For "T"'s in family situations where living a lie further frustrates and exacerbates the mental dichotomy, finding a professional who specializes in counseling "T"s is the ideal approach.

A well-informed and objective professional can help the "T" to define and understand her own feelings and then offer support and guidance during the process of "coming out" to mate or family. A third party, particularly a professional, can soften the blow for unsuspecting partners or family members. It is not unusual for therapists to schedule a counseling session with all parties involved for this purpose.

Even when the news is given by the "T" to her Significant Other, the availability of a professional can make the situation more palatable for everyone.

Who is the Significant Other?

Some "T"s want everybody to know who they are. There is a tendency to want to broadcast the truth to the world.

Common sense dictates that a lot can be lost and relatively little gained by having many others know about your "T"ism.

So while it seems very basic, one of the first rules in dealing with Significant Others is to decide exactly who they are. Who are the people who <u>need</u> to be told? Who are the people who <u>must</u> be told?

These questions represent a crossroads, the ideal place for carving a cardinal rule in stone, particularly for those who feel transsexually inclined and who plan to go all the way through the transsexual stages: <u>ONLY TELL THOSE WHO NEED TO KNOW ABOUT YOUR "T"ISM</u>. (One exception to this rule may be those cross-dressers who have found that telling many

different people about themselves is a way of lightening the load, that the more who know, the better the cross-dresser feels about herself and her activities).

This matter of self-revelation is highly individual. It depends in part on the ego structure and strength of the "T". Is she happier with herself being private or going public? In the final analysis, she is not responsible for other people's responses, only for her own actions. She must, therefore, decide what course of action will enable her to <u>live with herself</u> with dignity and integrity. Follow that guideline. It may mean telling some friends or others who don't <u>have</u> to know but who are a part of your world wherein the "need" to know determines the continued existence of the relationship.

During war or other perceived threats to security, governments have a method for dealing with secrets and classified information. It's called "the need to know." They only tell people as much as they need to know in order to get the job done, nothing more.

And that's the way it should be with "T"s, although it most often isn't. Only those who need to know, need to know for a specific reason, should be told.

Significant Others, wives and spouses fall into this category. If you, as a "T", are to live a full life, these people have a real need to know.

Do parents need to know? In most cases, no, unless a "T" continues to live at home (which is rare), or in other quite unusual circumstances. Obviously, if a "T" is going the whole transsexual route, all the way through corrective surgery to a new life as a woman, parents may well need to know. But even this depends on the age of the parents and the "T"'s relationship to them. We know a number of transsexuals who simply have not told their aging parents. They have maintained a telephone relationship or correspondence, but have not lived face-to-face with their parents for many years. These "T"s have chosen, for right or for wrong, not to "hurt" their parents, who ostensibly would not be around much longer anyway.

Those cases are the exception. Anything short of living full-time as a woman or going through the operation doesn't really warrant telling parents of the "T" activities.

Yet we know some "T"s who understood their parents so well, who knew that their "T"ism would be accepted and who consequently were able to develop wonderful relationships with their mother and/or father that included an explicit understanding and open acceptance of the "T" phenomenon.

Kay Metsker, in a <u>Tapestry</u> article entitled "Transsexuals and Their Parents," gives the most practical guidelines we've seen about dealing with parents:

Think through clearly what you want your parents to understand, then rehearse in your imagination a scene where you tell them. Notice, as you rehearse, any fears, feelings of frustration or anger, or your emotions that you are experiencing. Pay attention to your body also. Be aware of any areas of physical changes, like stomachache, cramps, headache, changes in breathing, tension along your spine, etc. Most likely you will re-experience old chronic areas of physical tension that you established long ago as a response to childhood fears of the adult authority figure that your parents represented.

As you rehearse and get in touch with emotional and physical tensions and fears, acknowledge them and then let go of them. This may take some effort on your part. Keep going over the same scene until you can do it without any feeling or reaction. It may take several tries, but don't give up. If you get stuck, talk it over with a therapist.

Only after you have completed this rehearsal and planning process should you approach your parents. Make an appointment to see them. Tell them you have something serious that you want to talk to them about, and ask when it's convenient for them to talk to you. If you can predict the amount of time it will take, tell them this too. If you set the topic of conversation and the length of time you are willing to be with them, then you are the one in control of the situation. Most important, you have defused the emotional bomb for yourself. After the first step, things get easier. So you will be able to direct the conversation and not be subject to getting hooked into old ways of being manipulated.

When you meet with your parents, start by giving them some idea of what you want to talk about.

A few introductory words such as, "This is hard for me to say, but I want to do it because it's important to be honest with you," will give them notice that you intend to assert yourself and are serious about it.

Then be direct and factual with your message. The simplest way is the best. You might say something like, "Mom and Dad, I want to tell you that I have felt like a woman (or man) inside, both emotionally and mentally, since early childhood. I am tired of hiding the fact from you. I intend to start living full-time as a woman (or man). If you disapprove of this fact, I hope that you will not disapprove of me. And if you do, then I regret losing your love for now, but I have to be true to myself." This may seem cruel, but it's probably more unkind not to face the issue and to leave your parents wondering about what is happening and yourself guilt-ridden.

Your parents will naturally follow the long-established patterns of dealing with you—saying no, scolding, or threatening punishment. These first reactions could even extend to vowing to cut you out of the will, or threatening to withdraw their love in some way. However, if you are prepared for the worst, then these threats will not work. You are standing on your own feet. No matter what the cost, you will have made a major step toward being in control of your life

and yourself. When they realize that they can no longer control your life, they will most often relent and accept you as you are. It may take them a little while to come to terms with the changes in your relationship. Give them all the time they need. Remember that you needed time to be able to gain the courage to confront the issue yourself. Offer them time to think about it. When they are ready and willing to discuss the issue further, be available to do so. You've made the first step toward redefining the relationship. It's now up to your parents to adjust their expectations.

Many parents go through a grieving process for the relationship that they are losing. Your parents may find it very hard to accept the changes. They've been used to the old ways longer than you have. They may greet the news with silence—a form of denial—or may simply decline to talk about it any further. On the other hand, your folks may surprise you and be far more receptive and supportive than you expect. There are those rare parents who have built their parent/offspring relationships on unconditional love (we'll love you no matter what), rather than conditional love (we'll love you if you live up to our expectations).

You should also be aware of the possibility that your parents may not be in total control of their own lives or selves. Your parents may fear what the neighbors, relatives, friends, etc. will think of them because of your situation. Your parents may need to build their own self-esteem and take control of their own lives, just as you've had to do with yours.

Keep your options open. Few parents are willing to lose contact with their children, and in time they will come around to accepting the changes in you and the changes in your relationship with them. Remember, change is always difficult, particularly where emotions are involved. It requires giving up familiar ways of doing things. Even if the old ways didn't work and weren't honest, they were comfortable, like an old pair of slippers. You may have a twinge of sadness at throwing away these "old slippers", but the old ways must go, to make way for new ones. Sometimes, the scary part is that you may not know what the new ways of relating to your parents are yet, and since you know the old ways so well, it may feel safer and less risky to keep them.

But it's worthwhile and exciting to move on to new levels of maturity. The second hurdle is still high, but easier than the first. Once an open dialogue is started with parents, it is easy to keep it that way. The benefits can be enormous. You can begin to relate to each other as real human beings. You learn new things about each other

and you may find a depth of love and feeling that you never knew was there.

There are really no hard and fast rules for sharing your identity except one and we repeat it: Anyone who doesn't need to know really shouldn't be told.

Telling children is usually not a good idea. Once again, in most cases there is no reason for the children in your life to know.

Yes, we've seen children who have been told from a very early age, or even as late as their teenage years. Many of these children are accepting, they love their parent and love her in any way she likes to live, in any mode of dress that she chooses to wear.

On the other hand, we've seen quite a number of "T"s tell their children, only to discover with pain and regret that their children could not live with the idea of their father being a crossdresser. We've seen families ripped apart, simply because the father felt a compulsion to tell the children about his "T" activities.

In many cases children find out about their father's crossdressing as a result of carelessness—feminine attire left around the house, telltale vestiges of make-up on the face, or inadvertent, possibly Freudian, slips (no pun intended). This method of finding out about the father's "T"ism is probably more damaging than an orderly, mature revelation by the "T" to the children in front of and with the acquiescence of the wife. Again, professional help is called for, if at all possible. Professional counsel is especially appropriate after the revelation has been made to children. Oftentimes a younger person will believe a professional's explanation of the "T" phenomenon more than he or she will believe the explanation of the parents.

The consensus of professionals on the subject of telling children is that parents should wait until the kids are grown. It can be confusing to children while they are working out their own gender identification, and it can also become an unwieldy burden for the child to have to keep that kind of secret from the world.

On the other hand, most "T"s and most "T" couples agree that if the child asks outright they would tell the truth. And that seems to be the best answer of all—the truth, but only when it's absolutely necessary.

Feelings of the Significant Other

Probably the most extensive work done with wives of "T"s has been by therapist Niela Miller.

For the last eight years Ms. Miller has been conducting workshops with wives of "T"s, providing professional counseling for wives and families and leading numerous seminars on the subject for families and professionals in the medical, psychological and psychiatric communities.

Some of her conclusions about working with Significant Others are particularly applicable at this juncture in our book.

After extensive review with literally hundreds of "T" wives, some of Ms. Miller's most pertinent conclusions are:

1)Most wives did not know about their husbands' "T" propensities before marriage, especially in first marriages (verifying the universal myth about "T"s that their compulsion will disappear once they are married).

2)Most wives feel isolated. They never talk to anybody about their husband's "T"ism, feeling that they are alone with their problem.

3)Many Significant Others feel betrayed about having an important secret kept from them, producing a lack of trust accompanied by a great deal of initial anger.

4)Wives tend to harbor a feeling of resentment about the amount of time and money spent on "T" activities.

5)Issues about self-worth and insecurities about their own feminine image surface. When wives are faced with the "T"'s idea of what constitutes an attractive female they begin to wonder if their husbands really find them attractive.

6)Issues of competition for time and attention arise and the wife wants her husband as a husband, not as a girlfriend.

7)The worry about being a lesbian surfaces along with fear about being "forced" into a sexual orientation which is not her natural one.

8)The biggest worry for wives: how far does he really want to go with this?

Ms. Miller notes that the revelation about "T"ism is often a catalyst that brings to the surface any weaknesses in the couple's ability to communicate. She believes that the couples who have done best in handling cross-dressing issues are the ones whose skills in the area of communication, i.e., listening, empathizing, negotiating, collaborating, compromising, et al, are better developed.

Ms. Miller also feels that the question of integrity is an important one. Bear in mind that the Significant Other is asking herself how much adapting and adjusting she should be expected to do. All of the research with Significant Others proves that it is very important for the people involved to be truthful with each other about their current feelings, concerns or questions. In Ms. Miller's words:

> Instead of being reactive and resistant to their husband's feminine interests, wives of Significant Others must take the time to really understand their own feelings and come out with a response that is honest and non-punishing as a statement of their current position. Both people must have patience and a deep sense of self and other with all the respect that implies. Neither person's needs and feelings are more important than the other's.

<u>What and how to tell her</u>

Telling the Significant Other can be a very delicate situation but if timed right and done well, the chance of longer term success in the relationship is higher, especially with crossdressers who enjoy being male.

Partners of "T"s at Fantasia Fair (held in Provincetown, Massachusetts each fall for scores of crossdressers and/or Significant Others) give some very practical suggestions for dealing with partners.

They suggest that rather than sharing the information at once it might be better done over a period of time. However, they agree that <u>some</u> partners might want to know as much as possible as soon as possible while others might need some extra time to absorb information.

The "T" partners came up with this suggested method for telling a Significant Other:

"I have a secret which I need to share with you because I love you and want to be closer to you.

I am a crossdresser; I like to wear women's clothes.

It has been very stressful for me to keep this to myself. I thought it would go way when we married but it didn't. That's why I didn't tell you until I was sure it wasn't going to disappear and I didn't want it to get in the way of our intimacy."

Alternative: "I didn't want you to suddenly discover the clothes and make-up and think I'd been unfaithful to you. I'm not interested in any other woman. I love you. I want our marriage to work."

"I am not homosexual; I am sexually attracted to you. My cross-dressing is not your fault. No one knows exactly why it happens but (in most cases) it starts when cross-dressers are very young."

"I don't ask for you to like or accept this, just to try to understand and support me. I recognize that it will mean stress for you as well and I am prepared to accept your feelings about it without turning away. I want this marriage to work and I acknowledge your right to be angry and sad about this."

"I'd like to share all the information and feelings I have about this with you. Also, there are wives' support groups and individual wives who will be glad to talk with you as soon as you are ready."

"Just as I am asking you to acknowledge my need to dress periodically (it will not go away), I acknowledge your need to set some conditions on when, where, how and with whom I dress. We will need to negotiate until we can find a compromise we can live with. Over time, our agreements may change."

Another suggestion on the part of these "T" partners was to give your partner or Significant Other books and articles on the subject to read.

One of the early books on the subject, one still in print, is the book written by Dr. Virginia Prince entitled The Transvestite and His Wife. While written largely from the perspective of the crossdressing husband, the book concludes that "T"ism can enrich a marriage if the wife will be more tolerant of the behavior. Dr. Prince gives some very practical tips on how to cope with the situation.

The book He: She: We: They was written by Significant Others (some of the same women who wrote the information above) at a recent Fantasia Fair. That booklet and all the others mentioned in this book, can be ordered as shown in the Appendix.

In telling your Significant Other about yourself, you might want to emphasize the fact that you will welcome questions at any time. Giving her the space to set her own rhythm of learning seems to work best. By nagging or forcing it on her you'll just create more resistance.

Some wives suggest that they got an idea about what was going on from the hints their husbands dropped before they were actually told. These hints included taking an interest in mail order catalogs of women's clothes, taking the wife to female impersonation shows or in other ways expressing an interest in things feminine.

"T"s who feel that they will eventually communicate their proclivities to their Significant Others might consider dropping a series of these hints. Because communications are so vitally important with Significant Others, particularly wives, a well-planned series of hints might go a long way towards making the final disclosure more acceptable to all concerned.

Without exception, the Significant Others urge "T"s making the revelation for the first time to continue to be sexually attentive to their wives, to make romantic gestures such as bringing flowers or in other ways letting the wife or partner know that she is still loved and that she is the partner of choice.

What can you realistically expect

Significant Others will have a diversity of reactions.

Let's look at the words of the wives and significant others themselves. From the booklet He: She: We: They come these words: "After first finding out that our spouses were crossdressers, we experienced a multitude of emotions."

Like most things in life that do not follow the straight and narrow way of thinking, when first informed of your spouse's crossdressing, you experience shock and disbelief. The fact that a huge secret has been kept from you, even though you may have known this person for many years, has a profound emotional impact on you. From the start you may deny it, not only to yourself but also to your spouse, but inside you know it's true. You may continue to deny the fact and then begin to feel a certain sense of guilt, asking yourself: "Where did I go wrong?" or "What could I have done differently?" But, remember, you are not to blame! This is something your spouse has been dealing with for a long time.

At times you may feel threatened by the fact that your spouse is now exposing a feminine side of himself and that he may not be the person you always thought he was. You also experience a great deal of fear and apprehension, the most fearful being the unknown and your naivete about crossdressing. The quest to know and learn more is a long trek on which you travel many miles of rough road. And every once in a while, you cry!"

Roger Peo, another therapist specializing in the "T" phenomenon, agrees with Ms. Miller's findings, but goes a bit further in his conclusions about the relationship:

When I asked the women how they felt upon first learning about their partner's cross-dressing the responses were generally more negative than positive. Many chose such words as afraid, angry, hurt, and threatened as well as expressing fears about homosexuality—both theirs and their partner's. Many women were also curious and displayed a supportive attitude. There were also a substantial number of women who were confused about the whole issue. With time, many

of these women appeared to have adapted to the situation so that, at the time of the study, many reported being supportive while reporting less anger and confusion. It appeared that the more sensitive the male was to his partner's situation and the earlier in the relationship he told her, the more likely it was that she would be tolerant of his behavior—assuming she stayed at all. When the women were asked if they had ever thought about leaving the relationship because of their partner's cross-dressing, 33 had never considered it whereas 17 had considered leaving at some time and 5 were uncertain whether or not to leave.

Why did these women stay in the relationship? There seemed to be two major reasons. Primarily, the women said they loved their partners. This love enabled them to be supportive of his needs, even though it was often painful.

Most of the women would rather that their partner did not cross-dress, but came to understand that the cross-dressing was an unchangeable part of his personality. Second, there were social and economic conditions that tended to keep some women in the relationship. Some of the women in my study appeared to have an economic or social dependence on their partner. Also, divorce is neither simple nor inexpensive and what can be given as the reason, especially if the marriage appears outwardly sound?"

Richard Docter, in his book <u>Transvestites and Transsexuals</u>, says "The most frequent themes reported in our survey (of "T" wives) were feelings of surprise, distaste, uncertainty, confusion, and a fear that crossdressing must somehow relate to homosexuality." Docter says that various survival tactics are used by "T"s and their Significant Others and concludes that, "marital success is obviously not dependent merely upon how the crossdressing is managed. More important is the basic character of the marital relationship and the quality of personal adjustment seen in the partners as well as their commitment to each other."

It is important to note that the issues for the wife or Significant Other of a crossdresser are not as severe as those that confront the wife or Significant Other of a transsexual-transgenderist. This distinction needs more emphasis, especially in light of the fact that many "T"s are not certain how far they will eventually proceed on their "T" trip. Because a majority of those reading this book will not pursue a full-time life as a woman, greater emphasis is placed on the Significant Other or wife of the crossdresser. Still, all of the opinions expressed are even more applicable, if possible, to the wife of a potential "T", transgenderist, or transsexual.

Finally, remember that the overriding concern of Significant Others is (you guessed it) security. Once they are in on the secret, Significant Others join the "T" in fearing the consequences of discovery.

Certainly other concerns, including time, money, energy, emotional involvement, and the sex life of the couple are important in developing an understanding. But security—the fear of embarrassment, the fear of discovery—still seems to be the number one fear of Significant Others.

If you are able to allay that fear at the time of revelation, you will have a running start on whatever the Number 2 fear happens to be.

What to really expect

Despite the best of intentions, painstaking preparation and even the helping hand of a professional, certain Significant Others are going to respond in a positive way, others in a negative way and still others at all points in between.

What can you really and rightfully expect from a Significant Other?

Can you expect the Significant Other not only to accept your "T"ism but to participate in it?

Can you expect your partner to participate with you sexually while you're indulging? Is it fair to expect your Significant Other to help you with your appearance, to go out with you in public, to aid and abet your "T"'ing at every opportunity?

The answer, of course, is a unique blend of yes and no for each individual couple. Some significant others will play along, some won't. Some will occasionally, some will always. Some will walk out immediately. There's simply no way of knowing about your own Significant Other, other than relying on your gut-level feelings and instincts.

From the standpoint of the "T", Dr. Prince concludes that "T"ism can enrich a marriage if the wife will tolerate or accept it. While her book is obviously written with an emphasis on the positive side of the

"T"-Significant Other relationship, it nonetheless stands as the most frequently utilized source of information about "T"ism for wives. A number of wives object to the very positive outlook of the book regarding marriage and relationships.

Nonetheless, if you are blessed with that most perfect of "T" wives, you are indeed a lucky person. Your spouse will help you with every little detail, she won't feel threatened in the marriage and you will end up with a much stronger union.

Realistically, however, intolerant wives are probably a majority. But you'll know, you'll know!

You can help your marital situation by being sensitive to your Significant Other's needs in your everyday relationship after she knows of your "T"ism.

In the TVIC journal, Helen Thordsen gave her opinion, entitled "Your Wife's Rights":

My husband is a transvestite. I love him enough to accept that portion of his personality with very few reservations. In our 35 years of marriage, nothing in my husband's practice of cross-dressing has undermined my love for him as a man or my acceptance of this facet of his personality. However, from my experience as a "TV wife" and my observations of married TVs and their wives among our friends, I should like to pass on a few tips to the readers. These tips are based on more or less prevalent problems which can throw a marital relationship involving TVism off-balance. Some of these point-

ers I will make are drawn from admittedly minor irritations or annoyances; others are based on conflicts which can bear the seeds of destruction into a TV's marriage. I call them, "THE TV WIFE'S BILL OF RIGHTS!"

1.) DON'T CALL ME ROOMMATE! I have no wish to be your roommate . . . or your "sister" . . . or your "girlfriend". I am your wife and want to be treated as your wife, no matter how you may happen to be dressed at any given time.

2.) NEVER LET ME FORGET YOU ARE MY HUSBAND! Nothing will make me feel more insecure in our marriage and in my own femininity than for you to become carried away by some mystical "girl within" and forget you are a man and my husband.

3.) DON'T COMPETE WITH ME when we are in public and you are dressed! I do not mind your having a good time with the femininity you've achieved, but I bitterly resent any competitive comparisons you might make between your femininity and my own appearance. If others at a TV party are so rude to make these comparisons I want you to be on my side.

4.) DON'T ABBREVIATE ME or other women in my presence. Whatever nut thought up such abbreviations as 'RG' (real girl) or 'GG' (genetic girl) certainly must have a deep-seated contempt for women. Unless you make me doubt my own femininity by your actions or attitude toward me, I need no abbreviated reminder that I am a real girl. How would you like it if I called you a "RB", or "GB"?

5.) DON'T TELL ME TVISM IS 'NORMAL' whenever I might express misgivings about your dressing up as a woman. I threw the word 'normal' out of my vocabulary years ago when I found out that it no longer had any real meaning in a world where no two people are exactly alike. So let's leave such words as 'normal' and 'abnormal' to the psychiatrists, the psychologists, and the social workers who spend their lives pigeon-holing human beings.

6.) DON'T SPEAK TO ME OF HORMONES, either in citing them as an excuse for your being a TV or by talking wistfully of them as a means of making your anatomy "more feminine". I like your anatomy the way it is and I don't want you suddenly to start sprouting breasts. And, in case you have not kept up with the medical literature, estrogens can greatly reduce your sex drive, which, thank God, still contributes much to our marriage.

7.) DON'T TELL THE CHILDREN YOU'RE THEIR "AUNTIE" if they ever happen to see you dressed. They know you pretty well and won't be the least bit fooled.

Let me do any explaining which has to be done if such an emergency ever arises.

8.) TRY LOUNGING AROUND THE HOUSE IN MALE CLOTHES once in a while. I don't mind you donning a pretty gown or negligee now and then but a steady diet of it tends to get monotonous.

9.) DON'T ALWAYS EXPECT ME TO HELP YOU DRESS! It takes me time to look my feminine best when we go out. I don't mind helping with last minute touches but I just don't have time to supervise every detail of your transformation.

10.) LISTEN TO MY ADVICE when I make suggestions as to your makeup or hairdo or carriage. I want you to look your best whether you're dressed as a man or as a woman.

11.) DON'T WEAR MY CLOTHES WITHOUT MY PERMISSION! You have dozens of outfits of your own. When I'm planning using an outfit of mine I hate to see it stretched.

12.) PLAY FAIR WITH ME WHEN IT COMES TO OUR SOCIAL LIFE! I don't object to your TV friends or to going to TV parties so I expect you to accept my straight friends and attend their parties with no complaining about it.

13.) STICK TO THE BUDGET when you buy your feminine clothes, just as you expect me to stick to mine. Let's talk it over before you buy something expensive.

14.) TRY PAYING AS MUCH ATTENTION TO YOUR MALE CLOTHES as you do your feminine attire. I weary of picking up your suits and slacks out of the corners you dump them in, and I wonder why you seem to treat your feminine things much better.

15.) STOP MAKING EXCUSES FOR BEING A TV! If I manage to live with your transvestism, you should be able to bear up under it quite well. You might be surprised to know that, from a wife's point of view, a lot worse monsters live in this world than TVs, and I'm glad you are not a drunkard, or a junkie, or a compulsive gambler, any of whose problems makes you pale into insignificance by comparison. All I really ask of you is that you relax, be yourself, and be in love with me.

With a little bit of help from your friends

Based on the "need to know" concept, you probably won't be telling your friends about your "T"ism, with the possible exception of a close woman friend or two who are not Significant Others.

A personal Note: Having a few female friends who know about your "T"ism can be a psychological life-saver. Once I make it clear to women with whom I feel I can develop a friendship that I am excluded from the dating pool—once I make it clear about the type of relationship that I want—my women acquaintances have an opportunity to accept or reject the overture. It has been surprising to me how many women will accept the nonsexual connotation of the friendship. On the other hand, I've had a few who feel that they cannot accept my "T"ism in any way. So be it!

Perhaps you'll be able to get this kind of support from the more organized support groups such as the TRI-ESS Sorority, Fantasia Fair groups, or the hundreds of other groups that meet regularly throughout North America.

These support groups can be the greatest help of all when it comes to dealing with Significant Others. A partial list of some of the wives and Significant Others support list follows:

INTERNATIONAL FOUNDATION FOR GENDER EDUCATION: I.F.G.E., P.O. Box 19, Wayland, MA 01778 (617) 358-2305 (Special S.O. program at annual convention)

TIFFANY CLUB WIVES SUPPORT GROUP: TC-WSG, P.O. Box 19, Wayland, MA 01778 (617) 358-2305 (Monthly meetings, outings)

THE HUMAN OUTREACH AND ACHIEVEMENT INSTITUTE: Outreach, Box 368 Kenmore Station, Boston, MA (617) 277-3454 (Special program at Fantasia Fair)

TRANSGENDERISTS INDEPEND-ENCE CLUB: TGIC, P.O. Box 13604, Albany, NY 12212-3604 (518) 436-4513 (5-10 p.m. weekdays, 10 a.m.-5 p.m. Saturdays)

EXPRESSING OUR NATURE: EON, P.O. Box 6293, Camillus, NY 13031 (couples group)

CHI DELTA MU CHAPTER - TRI ESS: contact: Mrs. Marilyn Frank, P.O. Box 9192, Morristown, NJ 07960
(201) 663-0772

PHI CHAPTER: c/o D. Beeman, P.O. Box 2512, West Chester, PA 19380 (Friends & Lovers Outings)

BUTTERFLY COUPLES OF NOVA: Butterfly, P.O. Box 3234, Manassas, VA 22110

CHI CHAPTER - TRI ESS: Chi Chapter, P.O. Box 40, Wood Dale, IL 60190-0040

GENDER IDENTITY CENTER OF COLORADO: G.I.C., P.O. Box 11563, 3715 32nd Ave. Denver, CO 80211 (303) 458-5378 (Special rap group for couples, significant others)

DELTA OMEGA CHAPTER - TRI ESS: Dallas Chapter, P.O. Box 461103, Garland, TX 75042

NEUTRAL CORNER: Neutral Corner, P.O. Box 12581, San Diego, CA 92112

SOCIETY FOR THE SECOND SELF (NATIONAL): Tri-Ess, P.O. Box 194, Tulare, CA 93275

A number of "T"s I have known who have made special genetic female friends have introduced them to support groups. Even though there is no sexual relationship between the "T" and her close friend, bringing that friend to support groups helped the friendship to flourish.

We have found wives and Significant Others to be very sharing in these support group activities. It is gratifying to see just how many wives will work with other wives and Significant Others on a one-on-one basis. These wives can communicate their problems and solutions much better than the "T" can by herself. So don't hesitate to get your Significant Other involved in these support groups as quickly as possible.

Hormones and the operation

When some "T"s begin to head for full-time existence as a woman, the chances of successfully maintaining a Significant Other relationship are diminished.

It is a rare "T" beginning the female hormonal treatment who can find a wife so understanding that she will stick with it through the hormonal treatment.

From the physical standpoint, the effect of hormones on the libido (as described in Chapter 7) means that the sex life of the "T" and her spouse will continue to diminish.

Living full-time as a woman, of course, means that the relationship with the Significant Other is probably doomed. The final blow to most relationships occurs when the sex reassignment operation takes place. Every reputable doctor insists that the "T" undergoing surgery be divorced prior to the surgery. The union is threatened increasingly as "T"s move towards the final and ultimate transsexual step.

Expecting to maintain a marriage and/or sexual relationship is unrealistic even as one gets closer to full-time living and all it entails. Expecting too much is sure to be disappointing.

Conclusion

"T"ism is a maturing process.

One matures into it and a very few mature out of it. Everyone who experiences the phenomenon recognizes that it is all part of the personal growth process.

There is enough guilt associated with the "T" phenomenon to make it a difficult

process, complete with growing pains at best.

But to add to that guilt a secret factor by not telling the ones you love about what is nearest and dearest to you (other than your loved ones, we assume) makes matters even worse.

Taking your time, planning your revelation (before marriage if possible) and treating the phenomenon as an opportunity for two mature adults to grow through a marriage (if marriage is the Significant Other relationship in which you find yourself), is the only long-term, mature answer. Granted, it's easier to say than it is to do. As is anything really worthwhile.

"ACCEPT ME"

Can you dear friend On this or any other Occasion reach beyond Yourself and find an image An Icon of me That will fit your earlier Notions of your friend with whom you shared So much And whom you thought you knew Until I forced you beyond the bounds of convention normality And Good Taste by my association with you In war I would be shot as a spy. My protective coloration is not the uniform of convention Geneva or otherwise. But did I not make a charming Companion with whom you were glad to be? And did not the brilliance of our admiration, mutual as long as it was conventional, dazzle the Onlookers - on when we were Together so long ago? Last week before I betrayed you, and asked you to accept me As I am.

—By Jacqueline

Chapter 9

Going Full-Time

Transsexuals recognize implicitly that full-time brings something unique to their womanness. They openly state, "You can never know what it really feels like to be a woman until you go full-time." Full-time is a distinctive period when the final touches are put on the female role performance as well as a period of immersion in which habituation to the role facilitates the all important quality of naturalness. All in all, transsexuals regard full-time as a very special, almost magical phase where the inner essence of womanhood blossoms, and everything that had been so consciously studied becomes second nature.

During full-time a transsexual learns to perceive the world through the eyes of a woman and to interact as a woman. The inner development of the primary female identity and the transsexual subidentity is reinforced by interaction in their new role. Feedback from their social environment encourages their self-concept as females. Through interaction with a new system, where they are related to more and more as women, they discover some aspects of a female world view they had not encountered before.

—Anne Bolin

In Search of Eve
It isn't easy being a girl . . .

You don't merely wake up one morning and say "Terrific! I'm going to spend the rest of my life as a woman!" and then do it.

Going full-time, making the transition from male to female and living in the feminine mode, takes years of planning.

Family reactions have already been discussed in a prior chapter. The reactions of your relatives, your friends and certainly not least to consider, your employer (if you have one), are all points that you will have (or should have) considered long before you make your change.

There are legal considerations, too. Legal records, bank accounts, educational transcripts, driver's license, credit cards;— the list goes on and on.

Somehow "T"s make it through the legal maze, although it isn't easy.

According to those who have made the transition into full-time living as a woman, overcoming obstacles along the way was well worth the effort.

Considerations
The major consideration that you will be making (or purposely not making) prior to going full-time is whether you are a transgenderist (a person who remains anatomically in one gender but lives in the life of the other), or a transsexual (one who will actually have the operation to remove the major vestiges of the male body).

Going full-time can be a testing period during which time you can evaluate exactly how far you want to go on the "T" trail.

Many "T"s opt for full-time living, then find that it isn't all it's cracked up to be. At first they may be thankful to have made the effort at living in what they thought was their preferred gender role, only to find in the long run that the "glory" of day to day living as a woman was not the journey of their dreams.

That's why the Standards of Care (see Appendix A) purposely call for the transsexual to spend twelve to eighteen months living full-time in the feminine role.

Many who go into full-time living do so knowing that they will never go the entire route, never get the operation.

This is perfectly okay. For many, simply living the role without the operation is completely satisfying. For these transgenderists, living in the feminine role is an end in itself.

How will you know when it's time to go full-time?
You'll know, you'll know.

That's a flip answer to a difficult question, but there really is no other.

You'll know if you've passed well. You'll know how comfortable you are. It's as easy, and as difficult, as that.

In general, there comes a time when you begin to feel like you're actually "in drag' when you put on men's clothes. When that happens again and again, it's time to consider full-time living as a woman.

When you find yourself having to make a conscious effort to "think man" you'll know it's time to consider making the move. When you find yourself sitting, talking, and acting feminine in a masculine situation, you'll be even further convinced.

Yet whatever your goal in life, you'll probably approach full-time living in one of a number of ways or with a variety of all, including:

1) <u>Easing</u> <u>into</u> <u>the</u> <u>situation</u>.

Many "T"s I know have eased into full-time living by dressing and appearing in public over a long number of years, getting better and better at it in their "trial" period.

At some point these "T"s live the part in longer and longer time frames. Somewhere along the way they realize that they are having no problem passing in the real world. Perhaps their relatives and friends have accepted them, and hopefully, their employer is amenable to them living in the feminine role.

A good way of easing into the role is one that is practiced by a number of "T"s we know. They work during the day as a man and immediately go into the woman's role at night when they come home, followed by an evening on the town shopping, nightclubbing, going out to dinner, socializing with friends or whatever else the regular woman's life allows.

2) Blocks of time as a woman.

Many "T"s who plan to go full-time manage to arrange for blocks of time—a few days, a week, a month or whatever during which they can live the part. Employment and other financial considerations will toll the bell in this transition stage.

Support group meetings, Fantasia Fair in Provincetown (ten days), weekend outings of the Tiffany group, and other organized group activities allow for dressing full-time in a controlled environment, eventually making it easier to spend larger blocks of time in the role.

A personal note: I was able to take approximately one week a month for many months of the year, then two and three week periods of time once or twice a year to prove to myself that living comfortably as a woman was possible.

Practice makes perfect. These larger blocks of time give you a great deal of self-confidence in living as a woman and they also allow you to become more accustomed to the practical difficulties you can expect to encounter on a daily basis when and if the full-time move is made.

3) The androgyne method.

As an androgyne you live your life "in between" man and woman.

You'll look and dress in a more soft, feminine style, than when you lived full-time as a man.

Perhaps you'll let your hair grow longer, wear women's slacks and blouses, perhaps a hint of make-up.

As those around you become accustomed to your androgenous look, you will ease even further into the feminine mode of dress. At some point, the transition from the androgenous look to the totally feminine persona can be easier than an abrupt change for all involved.

It has been my experience that the androgyne method sounds better than it really is. Although I know a lot of "T"s who have taken this course as they move towards full-time living, existence as an androgyne is somewhat confusing to those around you.

Anne Bolin, in her book <u>In Search of Eve</u>, says that most transsexuals or others living full-time, felt that androgyny "was a terrible way to approach womanhood. They considered it improper, unsound, and the antithesis of what transition was about. If full-time, transsexuals have the opportunity to become destigmatized as transsexuals and begin their full incorporation into society as natural women. To feminize themselves gradually leads to an unnecessary period of stigmatization. In addition, to appear androgeneously is to relate and interact with people as freaks or anomalies. An important facet of transsexual identity development as women is attributed to full-time status when they interact with people who respond to them only as women. That, in fact, is one of the advantages of separation from their former employment as men."

4) Cold turkey.

As many "T"s put it, going full-time is a very dramatic and symbolic event.

In their early stages "T"s often use the term "to wake up" or "to awaken" as a woman.

Simply doing it, just "doing it" one day (after lots of planning, naturally) is the route many "T"s take, with variations on the themes outlined above.

When the "T" does "wake up as a woman" she is fixing her place in the world. Prior to that time, even though she might have been working towards full-time, dual role passing was not firmly separated from the behaviors of drag queens and transvestites.

That first time "wake up" as a woman is a rite of passage that "T"s never forget.

What to expect

Expectations about going full-time depend on how the preparation period

mentioned above has been handled.

How others have been told, who has been told and the level of corresponding acceptance will have a great deal to do with the ease of the transition into full-time living.

Obviously, the transition will be easier if loved ones, relatives, Significant Others and employer have accepted your status as a "T."

It is, however, realistic to expect rejection. Not everyone will be as enlightened as your best friends, and perhaps some of your relatives. There are many homophobics in the world, those who feel threatened and insecure about aspects of their own sexuality. No matter how careful you are, some homophobics will read you at some point in time and react negatively. How you handle this type of situation is vitally important to your psychological well-being, perhaps your physical safety.

As a rule, the vast majority of people will not reject you; in fact, they'll accept you as they would any other woman. Remember that most people with whom you'll be dealing know you in no other way. You are what you are and they'll accept you for that.

One major problem will rear its ugly head occasionally—the "he" pronoun.

Even your best and most accepting friends will slip now and again and refer to you as "he."

You shouldn't take this personally but you will. We all do. People you've lived with, loved, and worked with, even the most accepting people in your lives have the memory trace in the back of their minds that you were once (and actually still are, anatomically) male. So don't blame them too much if they do use "he."

They'll get over that problem after a while. If they don't, it's their problem, not yours.

If you're the least bit paranoid, and we all are, you'll probably feel that the use of the wrong pronoun is an indication of what people "really" think of you. Could be. It's impossible to psychoanalyze everyone, but by and large the intent isn't evil or malicious and the slip is often Freudian. In fact, most people don't even remember using the wrong pronoun. A bit of thick skin (no extra pancake, please) will help you feel better about yourself and your relationships with others.

Documentation

In addition to biographical editing, those going full-time will have to have documented female histories of themselves.

This means creating a paper trail of personal and social documents that identify you as a woman.

If you're going to work as a woman you'll need to alter bank, social security and educational records. As a full-time woman, you'll need to have conformity in your checks, your bank accounts, credit cards and a number of other documents. In short, you'll need to create a history of womanhood on paper.

Timing on this count is obvious. You will have to change your documentation shortly prior to changing your living status. As "T"s approach full-time or change-over, they pursue these document changes with a fervor. And most of the changes result from one initial legal change—the name.

Name change

Nothing else can be done legally until the court grants this request.

Laws differ from state to state, province to province, and country to country.

In effect, you are reversing the order of birth and adolescence by going through adolescence in preparation for the birthing process. Changing names legally is one expression of your new status, your resurrection as a legitimate woman. It also allows you to create your life history in your own image, that of a female reinterpreted and recreated through documentation. It gives you a hook on which to hang your female identity.

In many places you won't even need a lawyer to change your name. Typically, name changes are simple. Fill out the proper paperwork, provide a notarized copy of your birth certificate, pay a small fee and appear in court. Many "T"s we know did not use a lawyer to help effect a name change. Simply going to the county clerk's or equivalent office dressed as a woman and filling out an application which explains the reason for the name change will normally get the job done.

Many jurisdictions require publication of the proposed name change in a local paper or legal publication for a period of days or weeks. This procedure may follow an appearance before a judge in court. The judge, incidentally, will most likely caution you that the name change cannot be used for fraudulent purposes and may well place conditions on the name change (e.g., all creditors have to be notified).

The name change is more than the legal key to changing other documents. It's a psychological change, your first opportunity to live with a new identity as a human being. For many, the name change is the most traumatic part of the transition.

What about the designated sex on

certain documents? Will the name change alone be enough? Will it be enough to allow the designated sex to be changed?

Again, there is variation from legal jurisdiction to legal jurisdiction.

Driver's license

There are as many stories about changing the driver's license as there are people who have done it.

Generally, however, driver's license examiners simply want to get their job done. There should be no hassle, particularly if you've had a legal change of name.

We've heard stories from people who simply went into the auto license bureau with their new woman's name change, showed their former license (with accompanying man's picture), asked for a new license with their new name, and obliging examiners gave them the license (perhaps after tests), filling in the sexual designation as "female."

Masculine photos on the driver's license are replaced with feminine photos and the woman's name. Even if the "male" designation remains (and almost invariably that can be removed later with proof of the sexual reassignment operation), it can always be explained as a mistake on the part of the clerk.

On those where the sexual designation has not been changed we've seen it removed at renewal time when the examiner notices it. It is explained away as a mistake on the part of the previous clerk or license examiner.

Passport

Passports are usually a bit more difficult to change but again, persistence pays. A copy of the court-ordered name change and a new picture will get you a new passport although the "sex-M" will probably remain. Not until you've actually had the operation will you be able to change the sex designation on your passport.

A clerk at the passport office issued my male passport, but accidentally typed "F." If I get around to getting a new passport and my new name, that ought to make the procedure a little bit easier. Everybody's entitled to a lucky break now and then.

Virginia Prince, the "grand-dame" of the "T" phenomenon, makes a good suggestion: If you wish to travel as a woman, get a passport made out to your masculine name aka your feminine name. As Virginia says: "The trick is in the photographs. You will have to have one taken that is sort of half-way between a man and a woman. For example, leave off the make-up and jewelry and wear men's or at least not too feminine glasses (if you customarily wear glasses), friz your hair out in the style that is part hippie and part wind-blown careless woman, and wear a colorful print blouse. If you get a cooperative photographer you can probably take several different blouses to the photography session, or several pairs of glasses and try different shots with various hair, blouse and glasses combinations. Select from the proofs the one that looks like you as a woman (yet something like a man) and send it in. The chances are they will pass it. If the picture is too feminine they will reject it because it does not go with a masculine name. Again this information comes from the author's personal experience with the passport office."

Dr. Prince in her book How to be a Woman though Male, adds that "as far as presentation of such a passport abroad (both literally and figuratively) no problems were encountered. Customs inspectors both overseas and home give it and you a pretty casual glance and return the passport. However, if trouble is encountered in the form of a question or two you can just say that you are a performer or public speaker in this role, and that is usually sufficient."

Financial documentation

You'll soon find that you're going to need a number of copies made of the court order that documents your new name change.

You'll probably have at least one savings and/or checking account. Because most businesses will want to see some identification when you write a check, you won't want to have your old name on the checks or the account.

You'll have to give your bank or financial institution a copy of the name change.

You may, instead, want to keep a bank account in your old name or simply add your name to your present accounts. You may need to cash a check in your old name at some point in time so it's not a bad idea to keep the account in both names.

Still, you'll want to have your checks printed with your new name, a thrill in itself.

Of course opening up a new account, particularly at a different financial institution, is a much easier procedure. Simply show your ID, choose your checks, deposit your money, apply for check guarantee and automatic teller cards and you're off to the races (or the shopping malls, as it were).

Armed with your new name, personal identification, checking or savings account in your new persona, you will be able to make the remainder of the changes needed.

For changing credit cards, send a copy of the name change to the company and ask them to change their files and issue a card in your name. This may be difficult to accomplish, particularly with financial files in a credit bureau.

A little search will yield a credit company that will accept your new name, particularly if you've made some charges in the new name. It's not a bad idea to open up charge accounts in a number of stores, anywhere that you can begin to establish credit in your new name.

By going through this process, you will experience a problem that many women have encountered. It is difficult for women, particularly divorcees, to open up credit accounts in their own names, on their own right. But a bit of patience and a dash of righteous indignation will accomplish wonders should you be hassled. You have a right to your credit as much as anyone else.

Your automobile registration and title will have to be changed. You can find out about this the hard way when and if you're stopped by a police officer, so you might as well avoid the unnecessary hassle.

By sending a copy of the car registration to your state or provincial automobile administration unit you can get the title registered in your new name.

NOTE: If you drive a car you would do well to get an auto club membership as a woman so that you can call for service in inconvenient places and situations. It is somewhat more awkward to change a tire as a woman, to thumb a ride for a can of gasoline, to start a flooded car in the rain, ad infinitum.

Laws in each jurisdiction vary, but getting an attorney to have real estate or other property titles changed over to your new name should not be too difficult.

College transcripts

You'll want to change your educational records, particularly if you plan to use them in gaining new employment.

Colleges and universities are used to this and they are normally very cooperative. If the sex is stated in the transcript, colleges will typically change it to female simply by receiving a copy of your court order, the year of your graduation or the years of school attended.

Chances are you won't be issued a new diploma. If your diploma is printed with your male name you're probably stuck with it. If you find that you're going to be checked on further back than college, you might go through the same procedure with your high school or prep school records.

If you were in the military you'll need to get those records changed. Generally, military personnel offices are cooperative. Again, the court order is all that is needed to effect this change in most cases.

Two of the most vital records you'll need to change are those kept by Social Security and the Internal Revenue Service.

Social Security is easy enough; simply send in the court order requesting a new name change and your new Social Security card will come in the mail a few weeks later. The clerks at the Social Security offices don't really care what your name is as long as they can get their work done. There are apparently no restrictions at the Social Security offices on name changes.

The IRS is a different matter. Here's where you might want to use an accountant as well as an attorney. It might take some time to change your name with the IRS, but again, persistence will pay. You might start at your local IRS office with your name change document.

Work histories might be more difficult to change. How you handle that will be up to you, and methods vary in almost every case.

Generally, we've found that most "T"s who are living full-time and have gone through the name change process have relatively little trouble changing their biographical trail, if they simply keep at it. Nothing happens overnight and nothing is irreversible. In the long run if you've gone this far it'll undoubtedly be worth the trouble.

The working woman

Entire books have been written about how to achieve the transformation, how to go full-time and keep your present job or move to a new position.

There are arguments for and against both choices. Those arguments are so obvious that we won't belabor them other than to say that every "T" will have to make her own choice as to which will be easiest. There are so many other considerations (family, financial stability, small town versus large town, et al) that the decision will have to be made on a case by case basis.

If there is an ideal, it is probably to take new employment where one is known as a woman from day one. For the sake of everyone's comfort, establishing a feminine identity from the very beginning seems to make the transition easier and more complete.

There are a number of jobs that lend themselves to the "new woman." A friend of mine, for example, had a real estate license in her masculine name. When she had her name changed she simply had the Real Estate Board change her license to reflect her new, feminine name.

By going to a different part of her large city and working with the real estate firm there in her new name, she found that the totally different environment allowed her to keep her profession, do what she did best, but do it as a woman. Real estate and other types of businesses lend themselves to this type of mobility.

However, for many "T"s who go full-time, finding a job is not so simple.

If "T"s expect to go through surgery, then they really must work as women, assuming that they need to work (as the vast majority of us do). Another rationale for working and living as a woman prior to surgery is to allow for a period of adjustment to womens' wages. Like it or not, women generally earn less than men, even for performing the same jobs. Figures are well documented on that point, but looking for a job as a woman will prove it to you on a personal basis.

If you left your previous job (where you were working as a man) with grace and tact, getting references for a new job should be no particular problem. Paving the way while still working for your former employer, asking for his or her help in future references, can be a big plus on the "T" job hunt.

Jobs which require a physical examination are usually avoided by "T"s, for obvious reasons. One minor problem in filling out medical history questionnaires for new jobs is how to answer questions about menstrual periods and other uniquely female health-related queries. There is usually no way around it. "T"s either have to lie, giving approximate cycle information or using medical excuses such as a hysterectomy. This is not much of a problem, since "T"s are generally well-read on the subject of female biology. By reading and questioning their genetic women friends about the subject they become experts on women's cycles and on "female" health problems.

After employment is secured, a "T" finds it very satisfying to be treated as a woman at work. Usually female friendships build, networks develop and work situations become very positive experiences.

Again, however, the "T" must remain always alert and stick with her story. She'll be asked personal questions about her past on subjects such as children, divorce, and marriage. An early hysterectomy can explain the absence of children, and various other gaps in female history can be covered. If your story is consistent you will continue to establish a credible female history in the minds of co-workers and employers.

Personal relationships
As "T"s integrate into society as women they tend to develop new social networks.

In retrospect, they find that their former status as part-time women was a period of loneliness. In going full-time, the "T" finds herself forming relationships, meeting new people, sharing more of herself and making some fundamental decisions about relationships.

One of the first decisions that most "T"s make, oftentimes unconsciously, is their sexual choice. Going full-time opens up entire new avenues. The desire to find someone to love and care for, someone of either sex depending on the "T"'s inclination, is a major decision.

In forming relationships, "T"s are faced with another critical decision after they've determined their sexual preference. Should they share their past with people who hold the promise of becoming intimates? Dating and intimacy are difficult for full-time "T"s, so difficult that some simply decide not to pursue close relationships until after surgery.

As Dr. Virginia Prince, who has lived in the woman's role for many years, says: "The individual should have encountered a great variety of experiences as a woman and handled them appropriately so that she has some feelings of being comfortable in the role. One only develops a personality from having great numbers of little, unimportant encounters with other people—both men and women—so that one develops a memory bank of situations met and handled as Jane, not as John. It's sort of like building up your own bank account with money you have earned yourself, not money given you by somebody else. Although Jane would always have access to John's memory banks she cannot depend all the time on his experiences and judgments in circumstances he has not experienced . . . Jane's personality, self-confidence and even identity don't come from just putting on a dress and lipstick. They come from the accumulation of a great many little interactions met and mastered by Jane herself so that she has a fund of experience to draw on. The periods of weeks or couple of months that she should have "lived" prior to the commitment to the full-time woman's life will give her this training as well as the proof that she "can make it."

Chapter 10

The Operation

Very few "T"s will ever have sexual reassignment operation.

That is probably as it should be. "True" transsexuals are a rarity.

Estimates indicate that there have been somewhere between 6,000 and 15,000 sexual reassignment surgeries in all of recorded history. When the total population of the world is considered, that represents a miniscule percentage.

Doubtless there are many "T"s who have gone through the reassignment process to its conclusion who now wish they had not done so.

On the other hand, there are many successful cases of total transition through the sexual reassignment surgery which, at least according to the participants themselves, have created a more well-adjusted person in society.

The purpose of this chapter is not to encourage or discourage anyone from going through with the surgery. Nor is it to describe in vivid detail what takes place in the surgery.

Because this book aspires to cover the complete spectrum, from masculine to feminine and all points in between, it would be a serious error of omission not to mention the procedures that the transsexual must follow prior to eventual surgery.

The surgery
In simplest terms, male to female surgeries include:

· Removal of part of the tissue of the penis and castration.

• Vaginoplasty: construction of the vagina.

• Skin grafts for a more authentic female appearance.

Different doctors utilize different procedures to accomplish these results. Medical progress will undoubtedly standardize the procedures for sexual reassignment surgery in time. The body of knowledge on the subject is expanding constantly. For purposes of satisfying intellectual curiosity, not to mention the potential financial gain, an increasing number of medical professionals are learning about and offering these sexual reassignment surgical services.

Sexual reassignment surgery is major surgery. It is expensive, time consuming and often painful.

A list of what can go wrong with the surgery is formidable. Yet if the surgery is performed well, and all other physical problems fall into place (no pun intended), sexual reassignment can and does work out quite well. In fact, stories abound of postoperative "T"s passing as genetic women even with gynecologists.

So the operation can and does work, physically. It is a viable clinical solution for the right people at the right time, but it is not a cure-all. A mentally disturbed male is not going to be any less disturbed as a result of sexual reassignment surgery. Reassignment surgery does not solve all of a person's problems. Life will still go on.

For the "T" who has had the operation, who has come to grips with so many obstacles, the success rate is relatively high.

Some of the problems and obstacles to overcome include:

A. The emotional pain, most often far worse than the physical pain involved.

B. Rejection by family and friends.

C. Losing one's job status.

D. Unlearning the masculine and learning the feminine modes of behavior (dress, actions, voice, et al) which is time consuming, difficult and costly.

E. Experiencing reversed gender discrimination for the first time.

Perhaps one of the most difficult facets of the postoperative "T"'s brave new world is described by Dr. Virginia Prince in her book How to Be a Woman Though Male:

When you step out of the hospital you are a newborn person in many social respects, not just in your own feelings. You have no yesterday unless you wish to drag your former self around you in everything you do. YOU have not worked before—you therefore have neither experience nor recommendations. YOU have no yesterday so you have to start with the day and build something all over again. . . . It never enters the mind of a prospective changling how she would answer questions and face situations in which yesterday and last month or year could not be explained.

Criteria for surgery

There are five essential criteria that need to be dealt with before the sexual reassignment surgery can take place.
1. Accuracy of diagnosis
Detailed and thorough psychiatric and psychological evaluations are a must. Generally, a gender team of psychiatrists,

social workers, an endocrinologist, a surgeon and even the patient as an active member of the team must accept responsibility for the operation. The gender team should provide objectivity, backing and postoperative support for the patient.

An ideal clinical approach is the one offered by the Gender Identity Clinic of New England. This organization, in operation for over twenty years, has developed a procedure which represents one of the best outlines for the "T"s who want to pursue sexual reassignment surgery:

The patient must be unanimously approved by all members of the clinic as a transsexual person.

The patient must not be in active conflict with the police or have a history of a felony.

The patient must be over 18.

The patient must have lived, worked, and crossdressed according to the desired gender for a minimum of one year.

No psychotic patients are accepted for treatment.

Referrals can be made to any member of the clinic by outside sources or directly by the prospective patient. The initial workup consists of a screening evaluation by two psychiatrists, plus evaluation and physical examination by the gynecologist and testing by the clinical psychologist. Tests routinely performed include the Wechsler Adult Intelligence Scale, Minnesota Multiphasic Personality Inventory, Rorschach, and Draw-a-Person. The patient is then scheduled to appear at the next monthly meeting of the clinic staff, at which screening reports are read and the patient is interviewed by the entire group. Patients are encouraged to bring members of their families to this meeting to participate in the interview and ask questions.

Many clients who are easily discouraged or not seriously committed to the reassignment process are self-eliminated by these extensive preadmission procedures. Once they have been accepted, hormonal therapy is usually prescribed. Occasionally, a patient may be accepted for treatment but referred for further psychotherapy before receiving hormones. Patients may be asked to attend sessions of the Twenty Club in addition to psychotherapy.

Some patients who are not transsexuals are referred to other resources for treatment. Many candidates are extremely anxious to begin hormone therapy and are greatly disappointed if the clinic's decision is negative. It is imperative, therefore, that some recommendations for treatment be given and a definite direction be plotted for all patients. We scrupulously avoid total rejection.

Immediately after the interview with the clinic staff, we give all patients opportunity to meet with our nurse practitioner. Frequently the spouse or partner or other relative meets with the nurse as well. These sessions have proved very beneficial. Most patients are nervous during and following the clinic meeting; they forget questions they meant to ask or information they intended to impart. In a private room immediately adjacent to the clinic, the nurse goes over the clinic's decision with the patient. She often is able to detect severe emotional problems that may have been overlooked at the initial visit, when patients were on guard and putting their best foot forward. At her discretion, the nurse practitioner may bring patients back later the same evening to discuss matters of importance that had not surfaced previously.

If the male to female transsexual is accepted for hormone therapy, she (patient's choice of gender decides what he or she is called) is referred to the gynecologist.

Gender reassignment surgery

Upon completion of the minimum one year life test, a presentation is made before the entire clinic and a decision reached on whether to proceed to gender reassignment surgery. If a unanimously positive judgment is made, the patient is referred to the surgical team, which includes a plastic surgeon, urologist, and gynecologist.

. . . Of the postoperative patients, 98% have agreed that the highly structured treatment program and meticulous testing were beneficial in the long run. They felt that their decision to have surgery was correct. They admitted that early in the program they had wished for acceleration to the surgical stage and some had considered leaving the clinic in favor of therapists offering "no questions asked" surgery. In retrospect, most felt that course would have been disastrous.

Because the treatment of transsexuals is difficult and complex, only a multidisciplinary clinic is able to offer a proper therapeutic program. Careful selection of patients for hormonal and surgical correction is indicated to allow many persons with gender identity problems a chance at a reasonably happy life.

2. Motivation

Most "T"s who reach the point of actively considering the operation are so well motivated that they are willing to undergo almost any type of surgery.

These "T"s reluctantly accept the long-term program of psychotherapy and whatever else it takes "to get the job done."

Generally the "T" harbors disgust and contempt for any features of "maleness." She has read much on the subject of transsexualism, knows all the buzz words and has learned from her "T" sisters how to "act" and satisfy the clinical concerns of psychologists and psychiatrists, play their game as it were.

By and large, the majority of transsexuals who eventually have the operation tend to test more feminine than biological females on psychological tests. They want desperately to be viewed as normal heterosexual females and so are highly motivated to get on with the surgery.

3. Age

The age differentiation for a patient seeking transsexual surgery is generally between 21 and 55-60 years of age.

There have been a number of younger persons who have had the surgery, and even some older "T"s, as old as 65-70, have presented themselves for surgery. The majority (approximately 70%) of patients presenting for surgery are between 22 and 35 years of age.

4. Family support

The importance of encouragement, support and companionship during the postoperative period cannot be emphasized enough. It's crucial that a close friend or member of the family, with the patient's knowledge, agree to provide assistance during the important adjustment periods.

Having reassignment surgery causes patients to feel very much alone. All of the support a "T" can muster, from family, Significant Others and intimate friends, will make the entire procedure easier and more manageable.

5. Follow-up Care

It is important for the corrected "T" to be willing to present herself for periodic postoperative evaluations. Psychiatric follow-up is also vital. Postoperative adjustments, attitudes and emotions may yield data for interpretation and use with future patients. Monitoring them with the expert assistance of a supportive professional is crucial to the "T"s own well-being. It is understandable that the surgically corrected male transsexual would like to eliminate all the unhappy associations of the former male role. Neverthe-less, a certain amount of follow-up is essential.

6. The expense

It is not cheap to go through the sexual reassignment surgery and all it entails.

Medical costs are going up. High liability awards and the gener al litigious nature of society today demand that the medical profession protect itself. This means tests, tests and more tests, evaluation, interviews, and a very careful and cautious approach to the operation itself.

The prices for the operation itself, which vary from five or six thousand dollars to in excess of twenty thousand dollars, are really only the tip of the financial iceberg.

Constructing a vagina is often only the first step in creating the "total woman." More reconstructive surgery is often needed, including skin grafting to develop a more realistic looking vaginal area.

Additional costs prior to the point of surgery are formidable, too. Electrolysis, almost always necessary, can run as high as eight thousand dollars and take two years.

Breast augmentation can cost three to five thousand dollars (this and all the other numbers cited include costs for hospitalization and outpatient care).

Face lifts, eye lifts, removal of the Adam's apple and other operations to feminize one or more parts of the anatomy can run the overall cost up to many, many thousands of dollars.

Most "T"s who go through the total continuum manage to spread these costs over a long period of time. Calculating these costs in advance will allow conscientious "T"s to do some long-term planning.

7. <u>From the doctor's lips</u>

Perhaps the most well known of surgeons currently performing sexual reassignment surgery is Dr. Stanley Biber. This world-renowned gender surgeon, living and working in Trinidad, Colorado, has performed over 2,000 gender reassignment surgeries over the last 20 years. He was interviewed by Wendi Pierce. The interview was reprinted from <u>A Rose News</u>.

Dr. Biber's words shed light on the surgeries themselves and on the motivation behind them:

Wendi: Dr. Biber, How much has your technique changed since you started doing reassignment surgery?

Dr. Biber: We have changed it in about five different stages. Our early instituted surgery was horrible. When we first started, it was terrible, it looked terrible, everything was heavy, it looked heavy, but everyone liked it because it worked. It looked horrible so we've gone through these various stages. The result is the way it is today.

Wendi: How long have you been doing reassignment surgery using your current technique?

Dr. Biber: This technique, it's been pretty standard for the last four or five years. There are probably three or four variations being used by other doctors. It is hard to keep track—some doctors only do one or two such surgeries a year, I don't know too much what they are doing. There really are only three places doing enough reassignment surgery to keep up the experience.

Wendi: What is your opinion of the satisfaction achieved by this surgery, both psychological and physical?

Dr. Biber: Physical satisfaction is pretty good. After the labioplasty the patient goes around being very proud of herself. Psychological satisfaction, if we have picked a true transsexual then you have tremendous satisfaction. About 95% have orgasm and most of the patients we have followed are most satisfied. If we picked them right we have very little recidivism. I can count on one hand, since 1979, the number who have wanted to change back. Just one of those I actually changed back.

Wendi: When do you feel it's not justifiable to do the surgery?

Dr. Biber: If a patient is dying of AIDS or something, we won't do the surgery. If the patient is not a true transsexual, of course, we won't do the surgery, or if he is a schizophrenic, but occasionally we'll do a patient whose gender problem is the cause of the schizophrenia. Before I would do such surgery I have to have tremendous corroboration with the psychiatrist, to really know what's going on.

Wendi: Do you feel the surgery is justifiable for a patient who plans a gay lifestyle?

Dr. Biber: Yes, we didn't before, but several years ago we started doing them. We didn't really start. We got taken in. Then we started looking at their lesbian lifestyle and started thinking about the issue. These people were living very good lives, were very productive and were doing fine. Little by little we became convinced. If there is homosexuality in the population, why shouldn't there be homosexuality in the transsexual population. So little by little we have advanced our thinking. If a candidate for surgery comes in and is living a lesbian lifestyle, we don't discriminate against them. So there are variations, just like in the natural population.

Wendi: Why do you continue to do this surgery?

Dr. Biber: I have a great deal of empathy for transsexual patients. I've seen so many, I know them so well respectively and I know what they have to go through. I know how horrible it can be for them. I mean if you project yourself into their situation and see how terrible it is for them to live their lives without being complete. Actually, it is just like frosting on a cake for them to have surgery. But if I can do that for them, complete it for them and make them happy people, that's what I want. They are really great people when you come down to it and realize what they have gone through. These people have gone through a lot of psychological stress, and if we can help them and make them good citizens, I like that.

8. Assimilation into society

So the operation can be successful.

Establishing oneself in society as a new person, however, is a difficult proposition at best. As we mentioned above, there is no personal history so that the new woman has to begin again.

She had no childhood background as a girl so she must build experiences, encapsulating into just a few years what it took the biological female an entire lifetime to accomplish and assimilate.

Entire books could be written, and probably will be, on the "T" phenomenon of incorporating into the feminine world.

As Anne Bolin says in In Search of Eve:

"They can now confront a new system of social relations. The surgery is much more than just a 'technical affirmation.' It is a ritual rebirth: the birth of a woman. This symbolic birth follows transition. It will be recalled that the term transition refers to transsexuals' real life test. It is also a medical term for the period of cervical expansion in the pregnant woman prior to the final phases of expulsion: birth of the infant. Semantically, the analogy with birth is inescapable. Transsexuals are like infants, only in their case infancy follows their social puberty and maturity. Through the remarkable surgical procedure, transsexuals are symbolically reborn as well as actually reborn. The vagina is a testimonial to their lives as women, as are their new or modified birth certificates."

A lighter look at the process of social integration for the pre- and postoperative "T" was run in the "Transsexual Voice," written by A. F. America. It was entitled "Rules for Transsexual Women" (Because Your Mother Never Told You, That's Why . . .):

1. Try to shut up about it once in a while. . . we all realize it's really amazing and sometimes terribly draining, but there are other things that you could comment on occasionally, just to show that, despite your medical problem, you are still in touch with the rest of humanity.

2. It wouldn't hurt to develop a sense of humor . . . tragic comedy had its roots in ancient Greece, no doubt written by a pre-op.

3. Make friends—and keep them. At the same time, remember that all trans-

sexuals did not come from the same cookie-cutter. Never assume that because you are of the same phenomenon, that you are of the same mind.

4. Try not to take obvious fashion risks. No woman should, but some of us need to be reminded. You know who you are.

5. Never, and I repeat, never pretend to have diminished intelligence in the presence of a man to whom you are attracted in the false hope of becoming "his little fluffhead". We generally come through all this with our brains intact, not-with-standing current jokes to the contrary. This behavior generally irritates people, and makes them spit up.

6. Please do not demonstrate to me how your voice used to sound . . . EVER!

7. Relax a little. There are millions of misguided souls out there rolfing and self-actualizing themselves into a lather. At least you know what's wrong with you.

8. Stop whining. It makes lines.

9. There is not a single documented case of waking up a genetic woman after having asked God to do so the previous night. Develop patience. Don't stop asking, just be patient. She's very busy, but She will get to you.

10. You only pass this way once (no pun intended), why not pass in as dignified a manner as possible? If people laugh at you, laugh back at them. Learn to be happy with yourself at last!

Chapter 11

Conclusion

No individual is entirely male or entirely female. By examining the complex myths and rituals of the "T" phenomenon, this book attempts to encourage an exploration of Eros, the mysterious force of feminine essence in nature.

Every "T" is different, every "T" is unique, every "T" is an individual with choices to make about the development of her feminine self. In the end, every "T" must make her own way and set her own standards for measuring progress and fulfillment.

No "T" is better or worse on the diverse continuum of accomplishment in passing, living as a woman or by virtue of having undergone a total reassignment operation. The operation in and of itself doesn't equal femininity in the purest sense, and the person who has had the operation isn't any more feminine than her sister who retains male genitalia yet lives a feminine lifestyle.

As transgenderist Dr. Virginia Kransk says, "womanhood is something that is between the ears, not between the legs."

Ultimately, it is how we look at ourselves that determines how others see us. Femininity and our sense of ourselves as women grows from an inner well of feelings and sensitivities transformed into outward appearance, actions and behaviors. Feminine essence is not measured in hormones, by operations or by any other changes we might make to our physical bodies. Femininity is not fairly measured by cultural norms or expectations either, so don't let others judge you.

One Last Point

Sadly, we do encounter "T"s who aren't smiling, who don't have fun and who take themselves so seriously we wonder why they bother. Sure, we do what we do because in one sense we have to, but why deny ourselves the pleasure in it? Lighten up, Louise.

Ask yourself if you're having fun. If you're not, why do it? If you are, have at it, have the time of your life. You'll be a better woman and a better person in direct proportion to the joy you take in your "T" activities.

Appendix 1

STANDARDS OF CARE

The hormonal and surgical sex
reassignment of gender dysphoric persons

Original draft
prepared by: The founding committee of the Harry Benjamin International Gender
Dysphoria Association, Inc.

Paul A. Walker, Ph.D. (Chairperson)
Jack C. Berger, M.D.
Richard Green, M.D.
Donald R. Laub, M.D.
Charles L. Reynolds, Jr., M.D.
Leo Wollman, M.D.

Original draft
approved by: The attendees of the Sixth International Gender Dysphoria Symposium,
San Diego, California, February 1979

Revised draft (1/80)
approved by: The majority of the membership of the Harry Benjamin International
Gender Dysphoria Association, Inc. (1/80)

Revised draft (3/81)
approved by: The majority of the membership of the Harry Benjamin International
Gender Dysphoria Association, Inc. (3/81)

Distributed by: The Harry Benjamin International Gender Dysphoria Association, Inc.
900 Welch Road, Suite 402
Stanford, California 94304

Standards of Care; The hormonal and surgical sex reassignment of gender dysphoric
persons.

Appendix 1

1. <u>Introduction</u>

As of the beginning of 1979, an undocumentable estimate of the number of adult Americans hormonally and surgically sex-reassigned ranged from 3,000 to 6,000. Also undocumentable is the estimate that between 30,000 and 60,000 U.S.A. citizens consider themselves to be valid candidates for sex reassignment. World estimates are not available. As of mid-1978, approximately 40 centers in the Western hemisphere offered surgical sex reassignment to persons having a multiplicity of behavioral diagnoses applied under a multiplicity of criteria.

In recent decades, the demand for sex reassignment has increased as have the number and variety of possible psychologic, hormonal and surgical treatments. The rationale upon which such treatments are offered have become more and more complex. Varied philosophies of appropriate care have been suggested by various professionals identified as experts on the topic of gender identity. However, until the present, no statement of the standard of care to be offered to gender dysphoric patients (sex reassignment applicants) has received official sanction by any identifiable professional group. The present document is designed to fill that void.

2. <u>Statement of Purpose</u>

The Harry Benjamin International Gender Dysphoria Association, Inc., presents the following as its explicit statement on the appropriate standards of care to be offered to applicants for hormonal and surgical sex reassignment.

3. <u>Definitions</u>

3.1 <u>Standard of care</u>. The standards of care, as listed below, are <u>minimal</u> requirements and are not to be construed as optimal standards of care. It is recommended that professionals involved in the management of sex reassignment cases use the following as <u>minimal</u> criteria for the evaluation of their work. It should be noted that some experts on gender identity recommend that the time parameters listed below should be doubled, or tripled. It is recommended that the reasons for any exceptions to these standards, in the management of any individual case, be very carefully documented. Professional opinions differ regarding the permissibility of, and the circumstances warranting, any such exception.

3.2 <u>Hormonal sex reassignment</u>. Hormonal sex reassignment refers to the administration of androgens to genotypic and phenotypic females, and the administration of estrogens and/or progesterones to genotypic and phenotypic males, for the purpose of effecting somatic changes in order for the patient to more closely approximate the physical appearance of the genotypically other sex. Hormonal sex-reassignment does not refer to

Appendix 1

the administration of hormones for the purpose of medical care and/or research conducted for the treatment or study of non-gender dysphoric medical conditions (e.g., aplastic anemia, impotence, cancer, etc.).

3.3 <u>Surgical sex reassignment</u>. Genital surgical sex reassignment refers to surgery of the genitalia <u>and/or</u> breasts performed for the purpose of altering the morphology in order to approximate the physical appearance of the genetically-other sex in persons diagnosed as gender dysphoric. Such surgical procedures as mastectomy, reduction mammoplasty, augmentation mammoplasty, castration, orchidectomy, penectomy, vaginoplasty, hysterectomy, salpingectomy, vaginectomy, oophorectomy and phalloplasty—in the absence of any diagnosable birth defect or other medically defined pathology, except gender dysphoria, are included in this category labeled surgical sex reassignment.

Non-genital surgical sex reassignment refers to any and all other surgical procedures of non-genital, or non-breast sites (nose, throat, chin, cheeks, hips, etc.) conducted for the purpose of effecting a more masculine appearance in a genetic female or for the purpose of effecting a more feminine appearance in a genetic male, in the absence of identifiable pathology which would warrant such surgery regardless of the patient's genetic sex (facial injuries, hermaphroditism, etc.).

3.4 <u>Gender Dysphoria</u>. Gender Dysphoria herein refers to that psychological state whereby a person demonstrates dissatisfaction with their sex of birth and the sex role, as socially defined, which applies to that sex, and who requests hormonal and surgical sex reassignment. Gender dysphoria, herein, does not refer to cases of infant sex reassignment or re-announcement. Gender dysphoria, therefore, is the primary working diagnosis applied to any and all persons requesting surgical and hormonal sex reassignment.

3.5 <u>Clinical behavioral scientist</u>.* Possession of an academic degree in a behavioral science does not necessarily attest to the possession of sufficient training or competence to conduct psychotherapy, psychologic counseling, nor diagnosis of gender identity problems. Persons recommending sex reassignment surgery or hormone therapy should have documented training and exchologic conditions. Licensure or certification as a psychological therapist or counselor does not necessarily attest to competence in sex therapy. Persons recommending sex reassignment surgery or hormone therapy should have the documented training and experience to diagnose and treat a broad range of sexual conditions. Certification in sex therapy or counseling does not necessarily attest to competence in the diagnosis and treatment of gender identity conditions or disorders. Persons recommending sex reassignment surgery or hormone therapy should have proven competence in general psychotherapy, sex therapy, and gender counseling/ therapy.

Appendix 1

<u>Any and all</u> recommendations for sex reassignment surgery and hormone therapy should be made only by clinical behavioral scientists possessing the following minimal documentable credentials and expertise:

3.5.1.A minimum of a Masters Degree in a clinical behavioral science, granted by an institution of education accredited by a national or regional accrediting board.

3.5.2.One recommendation, of the two required for sex reassignment surgery, must be made by a person possessing a doctoral degree (e.g., Ph.D., Ed.D., D.Sc., D.S.W., Psy.D., or M.D.) in a clinical behavioral science, granted by an institution of education accredited by a national or regional accrediting board.

3.5.3.Demonstrated competence in psychotherapy as indicated by a license to practice medicine, psychology, clinical social work, marriage and family counseling, or social psychotherapy, etc., granted by the state of residence. In states where no such appropriate license board exists,

  *The drafts of these Standards of Care dated 2/79 and 1/80 require that all recommendations for hormonal and/or surgical sex reassignment be made by licensed psychologists or psychiatrists. That requirement was rescinded, and replaced by the definition in section 3/5, in 3/81. persons recommending sex reassignment surgery or hormone therapy should have been certified by a nationally known and reputable association, based on education and experience criteria, and, preferably, some form of testing (and not simply on membership received for dues paid) as an accredited or certified therapist/counselor (e.g. American Board of Psychiatry and Neurology, Diplomate in Psychology from the American Board of Professional Psychologists, Certified Clinical Social Workers, American Association of Marriage and Family Therapists, American Professional Guidance Association, etc.).

3.5.4.Demonstrated specialized competence in sex therapy and theory as indicated by documentable training and supervised clinical experience in sex therapy (in some states professional licensure requires training in human sexuality; also, persons should have approximately the training and experience as required for certification as a Sex Therapist or Sex Counselor by the American Association of Sex Educators, Counselors and Therapists, or as required for membership in the Society for Sex Therapy and Research). Continuing education in human sexuality and sex therapy should also be demonstrable.

3.5.5Demonstrated and specialized competence in therapy, counseling, and diagnosis of gender identity disorders as documentable by training and supervised clinical experienced, along with continuing education.

Appendix 1

The behavioral scientists recommending sex reassignment surgery and hormone therapy and the physician and surgeon(s) who accept those recommendations share responsibility for certifying that the recommendations are made based on competency indicators as described above.

4. Principles and standards

4.1.1. Principle 1. Hormonal and surgical sex reassignment is extensive in its effects, is invasive to the integrity of the human body, has effects and consequences which are not, or are not readily, reversible, and may be requested by persons experiencing short-termed delusions or beliefs which may later be changed and reversed.

4.1.2. Principle 2. Hormonal and surgical sex reassignment are procedures requiring justification and are not of such minor consequence as to be performed on an elective basis.

4.1.3. Principle 3. Published and unpublished case histories are known in which the decision to undergo hormonal and surgical sex reassignment was, after the fact, regretted and the final result of such procedures proved to be psychologically dehabilitating to the patients.

4.1.4. Standard 1. Hormonal and/or surgical* sex reassignment on demand (i.e., justified simply because the patient has requested such procedures) is contraindicated. It is herein declared to be professionally improper to conduct, offer, administer or perform hormonal sex reassignment and/or surgical sex reassignment without careful evaluation of the patient's reasons for requesting such services and evaluation of the beliefs and attitudes upon which such reasons are based.

4.2.1. Principle 4. The analysis or evaluation of reasons, motives, attitudes, purposes, etc., requires skills not usually associated with the professional training of persons other than clinical behavioral scientists.

4.2.2. Principle 5. Hormonal and/or surgical sex reassignment is performed for the purpose of improving the quality of life as subsequently experienced and such experiences are most properly studied and evaluated by the clinical behavioral scientist.

4.2.3. Principle 6. Hormonal and surgical sex reassignment are usually offered to persons, in part, because a psychiatric/psychologic diagnosis of transsexualism (see DSM-III, section 302.5X), or some related diagnosis, has been made. Such diagnoses are properly made only by clinical behavioral scientists.

---

*the present standards provide no guidelines for the granting of non-genital/breast cosmetic or reconstructive surgery. The decision to perform such surgery is left to the patient and surgeon. The original draft of this document did recommend the following however (rescinded 1/80):

Appendix 1

"Non-genital sex reassignment (facial, hip, limb, etc.) shall be preceded by a period of at least 6 months during which time the patient lives full-time in the social role of the genetically other sex."

4.2.4. Principle 7. Clinical behavioral scientists, in deciding to make the recommendation in favor of hormonal and/or surgical sex reassignment share the moral responsibility for that decision with the physician and/or surgeon who accepts that recommendation.

4.2.5. Standard 2. Hormonal and surgical (genital and breast) sex reassignment must be preceded by a firm written recommendation for such procedures made by a clinical behavioral scientist who can justify making such a recommendation by appeal to training or professional experience in dealing with sexual disorders, especially the disorders of gender identity and role.

4.3.1. Principle 8. The clinical behavioral scientist's recommendation for hormonal and/ or surgical sex reassignment should, in part, be based upon an evaluation of how well the patient fits the diagnostic criteria for transsexualism as listed in the DSM-III category 302.5X to wit:[1]

> "A. Sense of discomfort and inappropriateness about one's anatomic sex.
>
> B. Wish to be rid of one's own genitals and to live as a member of the other sex.
>
> C. The disturbance has been continuous (not limited to periods of stress) for at least two years.
>
> D. Absence of physical intersex or genetic abnormality.
>
> E. Not due to another disorder, such as schizophrenia."

This definition of transsexualism is herein interpreted not to exclude persons who meet the above criteria but who otherwise may, on the basis of their past behavioral histories, be conceptualized and classified as transvestites and/or effeminate male homosexuals or masculine female homosexuals.

4.3.2. Principle 9. The intersexed patient (with a documented hormonal or genetic abnormality) should first be treated by procedures commonly accepted as appropriate for such medical conditions.

---

[1]DSM-III — Diagnostic and Statistical Manual of Mental Disorders (3rd edition) Washington, D.C. The American Psychiatric Association, 1980.

Appendix 1

4.3.3. Principle 10. The patient having a psychiatric diagnosis (i.e., schizophrenia) in addition to a diagnosis of transsexualism should first be treated by procedures commonly accepted as appropriate for such non-transsexual psychiatric diagnoses.

4.3.4. Standard 3. Hormonal and surgical sex reassignment may be made available to intersexed patients and to patients having non-transsexual psychiatric/psychologic diagnoses if the patient and therapist have fulfilled the requirements of the herein listed standards; if the patient can be reasonably expected to be habilitated or rehabilitated, in part, by such hormonal and surgical sex reassignment procedures; and if all other commonly accepted therapeutic approaches to such intersexed or non-transsexual psychiatrically/psychologically diagnosed patients have been either attempted, or considered for use prior to the decision not to use such alternative therapies. The diagnosis of schizophrenia, therefore, does not necessarily preclude surgical and hormonal sex reassignment.

Hormonal Sex Reassignment

4.4.1. Principle 11. Hormonal sex reassignment is both therapeutic and diagnostic in the patient requesting such therapy either reports satisfaction or dissatisfaction regarding the results of such therapy.

4.4.2. Principle 12. Hormonal sex reassignment may have some irreversible effects (infertility, hair growth, voice deepening and clitoral enlargement in the female-to-male patient and infertility and breast growth in the male-to-female patient) and, therefore, such therapy must be offered only under the guidelines proposed in the present standards.

4.4.3. Principle 13. Hormonal sex reassignment should precede surgical sex reassignment as its effects (patient satisfaction or dissatisfaction) may indicate or contraindicate later surgical sex reassignment.

4.4.4. Standard 4.* The initiation of hormonal sex reassignment shall be preceded by recommendation for such hormonal therapy, made by a clinical behavioral scientist.

---

*This standard, in the original draft, recommended that the patient must have lived successfully in the social/gender role of the genetically other sex for at least 3 months prior to the initiation of hormonal sex reassignment. This requirement was rescinded 1/80.

Appendix 1

4.5.1. Principle 14. The administration of androgens to females and of estrogens and/or progesterones to males may lead to mild or serious health-threatening complications.

4.5.2. Principle 15. Persons who are in poor physical health, or who have identifiable abnormalities in blood chemistry, may be at above average risk to develop complications should they receive hormonal medication.

4.5.3. Standard 5. The physician prescribing hormonal medication to a person for the purpose of effecting hormonal sex reassignment must warn the patient of possible negative complications which may arise and that physician should also make available to the patient (or refer the patient to a facility offering) monitoring of relevant blood chemistries and routine physical examinations including, but not limited to, the measurement of SGPT in persons receiving testosterone and the measurement of SGPT, bilirubin, triglycerides and fasting glucose in persons receiving estrogens.

4.6.1. Principle 16. The diagnostic evidence for transsexualism (see 4.3.1. above) requires that the clinical behavioral scientist have knowledge, independent of the patient's verbal claim, that the dysphoria, discomfort, sense of inappropriateness and wish to be rid of one's own genitals, have existed for at least two years. This evidence may be obtained by interview of the patient's appointed informant (friend or relative) or it may best be obtained by the fact that the clinical behavioral scientist has professionally known the patient for an extended period of time.

4.6.2. Standard 6. The clinical behavioral scientist making the recommendation in favor of hormonal sex reassignment shall have know the patient in a psychotherapeutic relationship, for at least 3 months prior to making said recommendation.

Surgical (Genital and/or Breast) Sex Reassignment:

4.7.1 Principle 17. Peer review is a commonly accepted procedure in most branches of science and is used primarily to ensure maximal efficiency and correctness of scientific decisions and procedures.

4.7.2. Principle 18. Clinical behavioral scientists must often rely on possibly unreliable or invalid sources of information (patients' verbal reports or the verbal reports of the patients' families and friends) in making clinical decisions and in judging whether or not a patient has fulfilled the requirements of the herein listed standards.

4.7.3. Principle 19. Clinical behavioral scientists given the burden of deciding who to recommend for hormonal and surgical sex reassignment and for whom to refuse such recommendations are subject to extreme social pressure and possible manipulation as to

Appendix 1

create an atmosphere in which charges of laxity, favoritism, sexism, financial gain, etc., may be made.

4.7.4. Principle 20. A plethora of theories exist regarding the etiology of gender dysphoria and the purposes or goals of hormonal and/or surgical sex reassignment such that the clinical behavioral scientist making the decision to recommend such reassignment for a patient does not enjoy the comfort or security of knowing that his or her decision would be supported by the majority of his or her peers.

4.7.5. Standard 7. The clinical behavioral scientist recommending that a patient applicant receive surgical (genital and breast) sex reassignment must obtain peer review, in the format of a clinical behavioral scientist peer who will personally examine the patient applicant, on at least one occasion, and who will, in writing state that he or she concurs with the decision of the original clinical behavioral scientist. Peer review (a second opinion) is not required for hormonal sex reassignment. Non-genital/breast surgical sex reassignment does not require the recommendation of a behavioral scientist. At least one of the two behavioral scientists making the favorable recommendation for surgical (genital and breast) sex reassignment must be a doctoral level clinical behavioral scientist.*

4.8.1. Standard 8. The clinical behavioral scientist making the primary recommendation in favor of genital (surgical) sex reassignment shall have known the patient, in a psychotherapeutic relationship for at least 6 months prior to making said recommendation. That clinical behavioral scientist should have access to the results of psychometric testing (including IQ testing of the patient) when such testing is clinically indicated.

4.9.1. Standard 9. Genital sex reassignment shall be preceded by a period of at least 12 months during which time the patient lives full-time in the social role of the genetically other sex.

4.10.1. Principle 21. Genital surgical sex reassignment includes the invasion of, and the alteration of, the genito-urinary disorders and may complicate later genital surgical sex reassignment.

4.10.2. Stand 10. Prior to genital surgical sex reassignment a urological examination should be conducted for the purpose of identifying and perhaps treating abnormalities of the genito-urinary tract.

4.11.1 Standard 11. The physician administering or performing surgical (genital) sex reassignment is guilty of professional misconduct if he or she does not receive written recommendations in favor of such procedures from at least two clinical behavioral scientists; at least one of which is a doctoral level clinical behavioral scientist and one of whom has known the patient in a professional relationship for at least 6 months.

Appendix 1

4.12.1. Principle 22. The care and treatment of sex reassignment applicants or patients often causes special problems for the professionals offering such care and treatment. These special problems include, but are not limited to, the need for the professional to cooperate with education of the public to justify his or her work, the need to document the case history perhaps more completely than is customary in general patient care, the need to respond to multiple, nonpaying, service applicants and the need to be receptive and responsive to the extra demands for services and assistance often made by sex reassignment applicants as compared to other patient groups.

4.12.2. Principle 23 Sex reassignment applicants often have need for post-therapy (psychologic, hormonal and surgical) follow-up care for which they are unable or unwilling to pay.

4.12.3. Principle 24. Sex reassignment applicants often are in a financial status which does not permit them to pay excessive professional fees.

4.12.4. Standard 12. It is unethical for professionals to charge sex reassignment applicants "whatever the traffic will bear" or excessive fees far beyond the normal fees charged for similar services by the professional. It is permissible to charge sex reassignment applicants for services in advance of the tendering of such services even if such an advance fee arrangement is not typical of the professional's practice. It is permissible to charge patients, in advance, for expected services such as post-therapy follow-up care and/or counseling. It is unethical to charge patients for services which are essentially research and which services do not directly benefit the patient.

4.13.1. Principle 25. Sex reassignment applicants often experience social, legal and financial discrimination not known, at present, to be prohibited by federal or state law.

4.13.2. Principle 26. Sex reassignment applicants often must conduct formal or semi-formal legal proceedings (i.e., in-court appearances against insurance companies or in pursuit of having legal documents changed to reflect their new sexual and genderal status, etc.).

---

* In the original and 1/80 version of these standards, one of the clinical behavioral scientists was required to be a psychiatrist. That requirement was rescinded in 3/81.

Appendix 1

4.13.3. Principle 27. Sex reassignment applicants, in pursuit of what are assumed to be their civil rights as citizens, are often in need of assistance (in the form of copies of records, letters of endorsement, court testimony, etc.)

4.13.4. Standard 13. It is permissible for a professional to charge only the normal fee for services needed by a patient in pursuit of his or her civil rights. Fees should not be charged for services for which, for other patient groups, such fees are not normally charged.

4.14.1. Principle 28. Hormonal and surgical sex reassignment has been demonstrated to be a rehabilitative, or habilitative, experience for properly selected adult patients.

4.14.2 Principle 29. Hormonal and surgical sex reassignment are procedures which must be requested by, and performed only with the agreement of, the patient having informed consent. Sex reannouncement or sex reassignment procedures conducted on infantile or early childhood intersexed patients are common medical practices and are not included in or affected by the present discussion.

4.14.3. Principle 30. Sex reassignment applicants often, in their pursuit of sex reassignment, believe that hormonal and surgical sex reassignment have fewer risks than such procedures are known to have.
4.14.4. Standard 14, Hormonal and surgical sex reassignment may be conducted or administered only to persons obtaining their legal majority (as defined by state law or to persons declared by the courts as legal adults (emancipated minors).

4.15.1. Standard 15. Hormonal and surgical sex reassignment may be conducted or administered only after the patient applicant has received full and complete explanations, preferably in writing, in words understood by the patient applicant, of all risks inherent in the requested procedures.

4.16.1. Principle 31. Gender dysphoric sex reassignment applicants and patients enjoy the same rights to medical privacy as does any other patient group.

14.16.2. Standard 16. The privacy of the medical record of the sex reassignment patient shall be safeguarded
according to procedures in use to safeguard the privacy of any other patient group.

Appendix 1

5. Explication

5.1.   Prior to the initiation of hormonal sex reassignment:

5.1.1. The patient must demonstrate that the sense of discomfort with the self and the urge to rid the self of the genitalia and the wish to live in the genetically other sex role have existed for at least 2 years.

5.1.2. The patient must be known to a clinical behavioral scientist for at least 3 months and that clinical behavioral scientist must endorse the patient's request for hormone therapy.

5.1.3.   Prospective patients should receive a complete physical examination which includes, but is not limited to, the measurement of SGPT in persons to receive testosterone and the measurement of SGPT, bilirubin, triglycerides and fasting glucose in persons to receive estrogens.

5.2.   Prior to the initiation of genital or breast sex reassignment (penectomy, orchidectomy, castration, vaginoplasty, mastectomy, hysterectomy, oophorectomy, salpingectomy, vaginectomy, phalloplasty, reduction mammoplasty, breast amputation):

5.2.1.   See 5.1.1., above.

5.2.2. The patient must be known to a clinical behavioral scientist for at least 6 months and that clinical behavioral scientist must endorse the patient's request for genital surgical sex reassignment.

5.2.3. The patient must be evaluated at least once by a clinical behavioral scientist other than the clinical behavioral scientist specified in 5.2.2. above and that second clinical behavioral scientist must endorse the patient's request for genital sex reassignment. At least one of the clinical behavioral scientists making the recommendation for genital sex reassignment must be a doctoral level clinical behavioral scientist.

5.2.4. The patient must have been successfully living in the genetically other sex role for at least one year.

5.2.5.   An urological examination should be performed.

BIBLIOGRAPHY (References)

Sex Differences in Human Communications by Barbara Westbrook Eakins and R. Gene Eakins, Houghton, Mifflin Company, Boston, Library of Congress Catalog Card Number 77-77660.
ISBN: 03-395-25510-4

Language of the Sexes by Francine Frank and Frank Anshen. State University of New York Press, Albany.
ISBN: 0-87395-881-0
ISBN: 0-87395-882-9 (PBK.)

Gender: An Ethynomethodological Approach by Susie Anne J. Kessler and Wendy McKenny. The University of Chicago Press. ISBN: 0-226-43206-8 (Paper)

In Search of Eve - Transsexual Rites of Passage by Anne Bolin. Bergin and Garvey Publishers, Inc., 670 Amherst Road, South Hadley, Massachusetts, 01075.
ISBN: 0-89789-082-5 (ALK. Paper)
ISBN: 0-89789-115-5 (PBK:ALK. Paper)

Transvestites and Transsexuals by Richard F. Doctor. Plenum Press, 333 Spring Street, New York, New York, 10013.
ISBN: 0-306-42878-4

How To Be A Woman Though Male by Dr. Virginia Prince. Chevalier Publications, Box 36091, Los Angeles, California, 90036.

Understanding Cross Dressing by Dr. Virginia Prince. Chevalier Publications, Box 36091, Los Angeles, California, 90036.

The Transvestite and His Wife by Dr. Virginia Prince. Chevalier Publications, Box 36091, Los Angeles, California, 90036.